Endorsements

"Rikki does an excellent job taking the reader on a journey of emotions from agony to health. It is evident within the pages of her book that she has been on a journey to success."

Esther Julianne McDaniel
Author of *When Memories Leave*

"Rikki Meister's book is packed with honesty—rigorous honesty and raw emotion. Rikki's most powerful tool and gift is her written voice. This is truly a powerful story, as I could not put it down."

Lorie Miller

"Beautifully written, *A Perfectly Messy Life* is a raw and vulnerable look at a story so many others have but are too afraid to share. It was hard to put down once I started reading it."

Stephanie Mills
Author of *I Don't Share Cheesecake*

D0878451

A PERFECTLY
MESSY LIFE

his is a work of creative non-fiction.
his book are based on my memory and perception.
privacy of those involved, names and some details
have been changed.

Copyright © 2019 Rikki Meister
All rights reserved

Printed in the United States of America

Published by Author Academy Elite
P.O. Box 43 Powell, OH 40355
www.authoracademyelite.com

rved. No part of this publication may be r
tem, or transmitted in any form or by
, photocopy, recording—without the
er. The only exception is brief qu

Paperback ISBN: 978-1-675-2
Hardcover ISBN: 978-1
Ebook ISBN: 978-mber: 2019
f Congress C

A

M

Learn to
a peace
depre

RIKKI

Dedication

To my mom, Becky,

You have always been there for me in good times and in bad. You have helped me in more ways than you know. You are my rock. I will always be grateful for the help and support you have given me over the years.

I love you, Mommy.

To my darling daughter,

Even though we have our ups and downs, I am grateful to have such a wonderful daughter. You are a smart, talented young woman who doesn't take shit from anyone.

I love you to the moon and back.

Contents

Part 4: Learning Process

Introduction

Life was suddenly too sad. And yet it was too beautiful. The beauty was dimmed when the sadness welled up. And the beauty would be there again when the sadness went. So, the beauty and the sadness went together somehow.

—William Steig

THIS QUOTE SUMS up what it feels like to live with depression and addiction. People with these struggles live life one day at a time and can't always find the beauty in it. Beauty is in the eye of the beholder, and we can find beauty in darkness, in pain, in silence. This quote is a reminder that life is both beautiful *and* dark.

My life is worthless. I don't matter. I will never be loved. Unfortunately, millions of people think these thoughts every day. I was one of those people. It was a constant battle from the time I opened my eyes every morning to the time I finally closed them every night. The constant sadness was eating away at my soul and threatening to ruin my life. In the beginning, I didn't really know that depression was the cause of my pain, so I brushed it off. I told myself that everyone has sad days and not to worry about it; but through the years, there were more sad days than happy ones. I put on a good show for family and friends, though, so no one knew what was happening inside. Many events led up to my inner pain, but I can't pinpoint the exact time my thoughts became inexplicably negative; all I know for sure is that I didn't want to live that life, anymore. I was done.

If it weren't for my daughter and my mom, I would most likely not have been around to write this book. Neither my mom nor my daughter knows that they saved me; they *were* and *are* my reasons for living. And I am not in that dark place, anymore. Now I want to share with you my story: what lead up to my attempt to take my own life on more than one occasion and how I came out the other side happier and more fulfilled.

Writing this all down was tough. I put everything out there, and I am afraid of what my friends and family will think. I dug up memories I would rather forget. But the thing is, I didn't need to forget my memories; I needed to figure out what I have learned from each one. I faced my inner demons and let them go. I found my passion and am rewriting my life.

PART I
EARLY YEARS

•••• | ••••

The Accident

In three words I can sum up everything I've learned about life:
it goes on.

—Robert Frost

THE YEAR WAS 1994, and I didn't have a cell phone. I didn't have social media. What we had then were pay phones, pagers and Walkmans. At 14, I walked everywhere and didn't check in with my mom unless it was urgent. That is what we did in the '90s—we left the house in the morning and didn't come home until the sun went down. No one really worried about our safety. Our parents trusted that we were being responsible and that we'd make it home safely every day. Yet, that was the year my whole world changed.

Life was good...until it wasn't. It was early February, and it was cold. If you're not from the Midwest, then you don't understand how awful the winter is. Freezing cold temperatures, snow piles as tall as a house and ice covering windows, roads and cars. On top of the cold, snow and ice, it gets dark at five p.m., which makes it hard to do anything when you're a teenager and can't drive.

I was on a basketball team with some of my friends that year. My best friend, Sarah (not her real name), loved basketball more than life, itself. She went to every practice, but I liked to skip most of the time. I was at a point where I didn't want to play sports anymore, so I made different friends who I was with when I skipped. I tried to get Sarah to skip with me, but she never would.

To this day, I cannot for the life of me remember where I was the night Sarah died.

Sarah lived in a big house, kind of in the country. The activity bus dropped her off at the end of her road each night. Remember, it was February, so she had to walk down a cold, dark road with no lights to get to her house. It wasn't a busy road, so she always wore her headphones on both ears at full blast. That night, she had no idea what was coming for her.

Sarah was dropped off on February 3rd like any other night. She began her short walk home in the darkness, then out of nowhere, a speeding car swerved into her and sent her flying. Sarah ended up on the other side of the road, headphones still on and song probably still playing.

The car that hit her took off. I bet they didn't even look back. Instead, the man driving sped off and hid the car in his garage. When the cops found the car a day later, it was splattered with her blood, and her hair was still on the front bumper.

Sarah didn't die right away. She suffered. In fact, no one even knew the kid who was hit was her until the next day. As I was getting ready for school, my mom told me that some girl had been hit by a car on Sarah's road the previous night. I knew in my gut it was her. It was all over the news. I went to school because there was nothing to do but wait to hear who had been hit. We all found out it was Sarah during second hour. My friends and I burst into tears. She was still alive, but her condition was critical. Then the announcement came over the intercom during lunch that Sarah had passed. That was awful news to hear over an intercom. I remember hitting the floor in a panic, tears streaming down my face. I couldn't breathe. I didn't know what to do. I had never lost anyone before. She was one of my best friends, and she was gone. The whole situation was surreal. I floated through the rest of the school day in a haze. I know I sat in a hallway crying, and my teacher tried talking to me, but I didn't want to talk to anyone.

I took my time walking home that day. I still didn't want to see or talk to anyone. When I finally made it home, my brother was there waiting for me. He threw his arms around me, and I cried until I had no tears left. When my mom got home, I sobbed some more, but no tears formed in my eyes. I was mentally and physically exhausted.

It has been 25 years since Sarah passed away, and I still miss her every day. She was one of the greatest friends I ever had. We always had fun together, got into trouble together and made each other laugh.

1994 was a tough year for me. I had already lost one of my best friends, and five months later, I lost my grandma. Fourteen is too young to deal with so much grief. I had no idea how to process it, and I knew I had a choice to make. Deal with the pain, grieve and move on with my life, or I could keep my feelings bottled up. I chose to keep my feelings bottled up. I didn't deal with it, and I never wanted to talk about it. I was in too much pain. I didn't want to relive any of it.

My mom was there for me, supporting me, but I always said I was fine. I'm sure she was worried. I didn't tell my mom that much. I was a teenager and felt like she wouldn't understand. I also didn't want to give her more to worry about; she had enough to deal with. My mom worked two jobs to support us since my dad couldn't hold a job. My mom was working her ass off to make ends meet. The last thing I wanted to do was give her more on her over-full plate. I know now that I should have talked to her, I should have let her in. But I didn't know anything was wrong with the way I was handling it.

I kept moving forward with my life, but I found ways to numb my pain and grief. At 14, it's pretty hard to deal with your emotions, anyway. Add loss to that, and it's like my life was put on pause. There were support groups at school, but I didn't go. I wasn't going to sit there and share my feelings or cry in front of my classmates. That wasn't me. I decided to take matters into my own hands.

I had my first drink shortly after Sarah passed away. My mom had an old bottle of peach schnapps in the cupboard above the microwave. I used to sneak drinks of it whenever I could. It tasted awful and hurt my throat a little, but I drank it, anyway. I never got drunk from it, just a little buzzed. The alcohol made my head feel fuzzy. I didn't feel so sad anymore. It was taking my pain away. I liked how it made me feel—like I was on top of the world. Nothing could hurt me.

The choice to deal with my grief by experimenting with alcohol had major consequences. My grades started slipping, my attitude in school was shitty, and I didn't care. I started hanging out with the wrong crowd. I dated a guy named Travis for a few months. He ran with the stoners and drug-gies, but he was like, so cool. We used to get into trouble for making out in the hallways in between classes. He asked me to smoke with him a few times, but I said no. I wasn't ready to smoke weed, and he never asked again.

My mom couldn't stand Travis. When we had people over to the house, my mom made everyone take their shoes off. When my boyfriend took his off, his socks were as dirty as the ground, so he may as well have kept the shoes on. She hated that. It makes me laugh to think about that now. I'm pretty sure she thought he was a bad influence on me too.

Although my mom didn't know about my drinking, she knew about the bad grades. She was, of course, disappointed, and I hate when my mom is disappointed. It's the worst feeling for me to disappoint my mom. So, I worked to get my grades back up so I wouldn't get held back. I ended up with a C average in my freshman year, which I was fine with. I was able to move into my sophomore year, and that is all that mattered to me at that point.

I had learned at this young age to numb my emotional pain instead of dealing with it. From losing my best friend to a drunk driver to having my first drink at age 14, something was put into motion, and I had no idea what it would cause to take place in the rest of my life.

····· 2 ·····

The Proposal

Heartbreak is life educating us.

—George Bernard Shaw

I CONSIDERED ALEX (not his real name) my best guy friend during my sophomore year. He moved into the house across the street from me. We became fast friends and always hung out the summer before school started. Alex had this ease about him, like he was floating through life without a care in the world. When we were together, he looked at me like I was the only thing that mattered to him in the moment. He had so much energy, kind of like the Energizer Bunny; always on the go, never sitting still. He would come to my house to shoot hoops, and I'd go to his house to play the guitar. Alex and I talked and hung out almost every day that summer.

Things changed when school started. He was a senior and brand new to our school. He had no trouble making friends. Needless to say, once school started, I was kind of a backup when he didn't have anything better to do. He met and became friends with a lot of seniors from our marching band. We were both in marching band, but I wasn't friends with many of the seniors.

Whenever Alex asked me to hang out, I jumped at every opportunity. I wanted to be near him, he was like a magnet to me. For me, attention from a senior, even if inconsistent, was better than none at all. He would make plans with me and cancel at the last minute because something better came along. I would stay home and wallow, sometimes cry. I felt like I wasn't good enough for him.

My brother couldn't stand how he treated me, so he always treated Alex like shit whenever he came around. It always pissed me off when he did that. Now that I am almost 40 and writing about it, I have to say that my brother was awesome in that way. He didn't want me to get hurt, and for that, I am grateful. It was his way of protecting me.

Thank God I had my best girlfriend, Katie. She was always there for me, even more so when Alex stood me up, which was a lot. Katie and I spent a lot of time together, talking, laughing and cheering each other up. I called her mom "mom," and she did the same with my mom. We mostly hung out at her house, mainly because her mom still smoked, and my mom didn't. Her mom smoked in the house, and she didn't care if we did, too. Her parents were gone most weekends, so we had parties there all the time. There was always beer and other liquor, cigarettes, weed, and loud music. To this day, I have no clue where we even got the alcohol.

I remember at one party we had a Ouija board. One of the guys brought weed, and we decided to have some drinks, smoke some weed and call on some spirits. I still didn't smoke weed yet, and I didn't want to start. I was fine with cigarettes and beer. We started playing, and everyone got pissed because we thought someone was moving the piece. One guy freaked out and threw the mover piece across the room; it hit the wall and broke into pieces. Then he got even more angry when his girlfriend tried to calm him down; he started yelling at her and raised his fist as if he was going to punch her. Katie threatened to call the cops, which ended the party real fast. Everyone left except me, Katie and the asshole guy's girlfriend because we didn't want her going with him.

We had several parties at Katie's house. That was the only one that got out of hand. Most of the time we sat around drinking, smoking and laughing. Katie sometimes drank too much and would get sick.

I liked drinking because it took me away from reality for a while. Until the parties were over. I always had to wake up the next day to face the real world, again. Besides, I had a job at McDonald's, and I usually worked at five in the morning on Sundays. I never called in sick for anything. Well, one time I did when I was seventeen. I had gotten lice from my friend's two-year-old after babysitting her.

Regardless of all the drinking and partying, I still managed to have my job and keep my grades up. I got my job at McDonald's when I was 16. My mom was also working there part-time. I didn't want to disappoint my mom by calling in sick after being out with friends. She got me the job. I also didn't want to lose my job; l liked making my own money.

As for Alex, I fell for him hard, even though he treated me like shit. I loved him so much that I let him take my virginity. I decided that I was ready and that he was the one. He talked to me about it many times while we were hanging out. I cannot remember exactly how it happened or what made me decide I was ready. I loved him, and I wanted to show him how much I loved him. I was sixteen, and he was seventeen, almost eighteen.

After he graduated and moved away, we kept in touch. He wrote me letters from the military, very sweet letters. We wrote back and forth for the next year, but eventually it stopped, and I moved on. I kept the letters until I was in my thirties. I would reread them from time to time and get sad. I would always read the letters when my life was not where I wanted it to be. Reminiscing about the past and wishing I could have done things differently made me sad. Sometimes I cried and poured myself a drink. I was torturing myself. One day, as I was reading through the letters for the hundredth time, tears falling from my eyes, I decided I didn't need to relive that pain anymore. I finished reading them for the last time, put them in my fire pit and set them on fire. I watched as the letters turned into ash, watching the words go up in smoke. I felt a sense of relief, like I was closing that chapter of my life once and for all.

During my final two years of high school, I continued to party and drink. I still had my job and got decent grades. I was happy. I even had a nice boyfriend named Greg. I met him while Katie and I were cruising in her car up and down main street. Greg was very shy, but when we were alone he was always talking. He was very polite and respectful, much different than I was used to.

Alex came back to visit during my senior year, and I agreed to go to dinner with him. I wanted to see him, but I was also nervous. I was happy with Greg, and I didn't want to mess it up by having feelings come rushing back. I decided to go to dinner because I wanted to see him, again. We shared our stories, him of life after high school, me of my senior year. We talked for several hours at the restaurant.

Before he dropped me off, we sat in the car for a while and talked some more. He said he still loved me and asked me to marry him. He didn't have a ring but said he would get one. My eyes filled with tears as I considered my answer. I still loved him on some level. He didn't wait for my answer. Instead, he leaned in and kissed me. I kissed him back and then stopped, remembering how I had a great boyfriend. Part of me wanted to say "yes." I used to imagine what our life would look like if we ever got married. But I loved Greg, though, and he loved me. I wasn't going to screw that up. I was still in high school for one thing, and Alex treated me badly in the past, so why would I think he would be better now? So, I said "no," and I don't for one second regret it. He was disappointed but understood. He dropped me off at home, we hugged for what seemed like an eternity, he kissed my forehead and then got back in his car and drove off.

● ● ●

After my high school graduation, I had no clue what I wanted to do with my life. I wanted to work in a factory with my mom and make money. I didn't want to get a degree. I didn't even know what I was interested in. My mom and brother convinced me to get a degree in elementary education. I didn't really want to, but I also didn't want to disappoint them. I had to go to a community college first to obtain a transfer degree since I didn't take the SAT or ACT tests. Greg decided to go to school with me. It took two years to complete the transfer degree. The next decision was where to finish my teaching degree. I didn't want to move out of state, so I chose to move two hours south and go to a University in Minnesota. Greg did the same. We found an off-campus apartment to rent together, and in the summer of 2000, we packed up and moved to southern Minnesota. I felt like my mom and brother pushed me into making those decisions. I had to make something of myself; I needed a real job, according to them.

Living with Greg was exciting. I had never lived with anyone but my parents, so moving in with my boyfriend was awesome. We moved into our apartment a few months before school started. Greg had a two-week training for the reserves the day after we moved in, so I was all alone. I didn't know my way around, so I never left the apartment for the whole two

weeks. I was afraid I'd get lost. I spent my tir,
organizing. We had gone grocery shopping
left, so I was set for food, although I did orde
It was lonely in the apartment for two weeks
talked to my mom every night; she always ma
ter. Although I was lonely, I didn't mind being alone; it was
kind of liberating to know I was on my own for the first time.

Greg and I both got jobs at the same department store.
We worked different shifts, though. We only had one class
together, so we didn't see each other that often. We were both
busy with school and work. I met a lot of people at work and
school that I liked to hang out with on weekends. Greg never
wanted to go out with us, so he usually stayed home. The one
time he did come with us, it was awkward. He didn't talk to
anyone and just stood there with a beer. I felt so uncomfortable. I was trying to have fun but trying to make sure he was
having fun as well.

I wanted to go out and party, have a good time with
friends, and he wanted to stay home. Greg didn't make friends
very easily since he was so shy. I felt bad, but I didn't want to
sit at home, so I went out every chance I got. Greg only came
with that one time. The only time we really saw each other
was in passing at work and bedtime. I felt like Greg and I
were drifting apart.

• • •

I met Jason (not his real name) a few months after moving.
We worked together at the department store. We were always
talking and flirting at work. We became very good friends.
We even went out to the bar with other friends from work to
play pool and darts. I wanted to go out and have fun, even if
it meant that Greg wasn't there. One night while I was out
with work friends, Jason and I were flirting a lot. I remember
wearing these Lucky Brand jeans and a sexy red tank top that

,ed off just a little of my lower belly. Jason kept swiping
s finger over my exposed skin. It felt good to be touched
by someone. With Greg working nights and not wanting to
go out after work, I wasn't getting the attention I needed at
home. One thing led to another, and I ended up going home
with Jason.

I told Greg about it the next day. I felt like a terrible person as I wasn't the cheating type. I hated myself for doing it,
but our relationship wasn't working. I was tired of him not
wanting to come out with me. I was tired of him not making
any friends or even trying to get to know mine. I was even
tired of coming home to him. The little things were starting to annoy me. He didn't keep up with his half of the rent,
didn't clean the apartment, and didn't keep up with his laundry. We decided to break up, and I moved out a few months
later when our lease was up.

I was ready to move on from my high school relationship
and start living the college life. I wanted to drink, party and
have fun. I also wanted a boyfriend who wanted to spend
time with me and have fun with me, so I moved on.

·····3·····

Life as a Mother

He that shuts love out, in turn, shall be shut out from love.

—Alfred, Lord Tennyson

I MOVED IN with Jason after Greg and I broke up. We lived in his mobile home for about six months while making plans to build a house. We were moving fast, too fast. We were young and in love. During the building of our house, I found out I was pregnant. Jason was ecstatic; I was scared. I wasn't ready to be a mom. I was still in school and felt I was way too young. But seeing him so happy made me happy, so I decided to have the baby. I may not have been ready to be a mom, but Jason was ready to be a dad.

Being pregnant turned out to be a blessing for me. I gave up drinking and smoking during my pregnancy and didn't pick either habit up again for two years after her birth. When I did start drinking again, at first I only drank a beer or two, here and there. I only smoked on occasion when I was out with friends.

Our daughter was born in September of 2002. When I met her, I fell in love immediately. It was a weird feeling to love someone so much that you just met. She was my angel. Jason was a good dad. He helped with our daughter all the time. In fact, he did most of the baby stuff for the first few weeks. I was scared to change her diaper. I thought I would break her. It didn't take long for me to fall into motherhood, but I am glad Jason was there to help and support me. I was also glad that my mom stayed with us for a week after she was born. My mom helped me figure out how to be a mother by showing me how she did things when I was a baby, as well as figuring out what my daughter needed when I had no clue.

After my mom went back home, I was still pretty nervous about motherhood. Jason did a lot, but he also had a daycare in our basement to run. Jason's sister was training to be a doula, so I was her practice client. She was so helpful. Anytime I felt like I was screwing up, I would call her, and she would come over right away. She helped me through my tough times as well as my good times. She made sure I knew that I wasn't the only mother who had a hard time with their baby.

Our daughter Isobelle was a handful as soon as she turned two. She developed a very unique personality. Isobelle was and is very headstrong and always right. When she was two, she started having screaming tantrums if she didn't get her way. I remember one time she was on a time out; she proceeded to throw things against her walls as well as kick them. She was screaming at the top of her lungs and balling. Her face was bright red and tear stained. I couldn't calm her down; when I tried, she would kick me and yell louder. I had to take everything out of her room because I was scared she would break something and hurt herself. That didn't stop her from slamming her heels into the wall, though. I had no idea what to do, so I walked away and let her scream it out alone. It took about an hour for her to calm down. Isobelle had many episodes like this in her childhood. It was putting a strain on both Jason and me. Jason would get mad when I would try to discipline her; he said it made it worse. Jason never disciplined her, which didn't work, either.

I was finishing up my teaching degree at that time. I had one semester left which involved student teaching. I was so excited to graduate and get a full-time teaching job. I was very hopeful that I would find one right away. I graduated in December of 2004 and started applying for jobs for the upcoming 2005/2006 school year. I knew I wouldn't get a full-time job in January of 2005 because it was the middle of the year, so I started substitute teaching. I was called for many interviews for the new school year in many different school districts. I was not offered any of the jobs. I didn't have enough experience yet, so no district wanted me. I would call my mom crying after each rejection phone call, and she would talk me down and encourage me to keep trying. Not getting a teaching job for the upcoming year brought more tension into my marriage. Jason wanted to be able to quit his job as a daycare provider, so when I didn't get a job as a teacher; not only was I frustrated and upset, I had a husband who was angry and annoyed every time I wasn't offered a job.

Our marriage started getting even worse when I became close friends with the neighbor. Abby (not her real name) and I hung out all the time. She was my best friend in town and the only one I could talk to about anything. Sometimes we sat and talked for hours smoking cigarettes. I think Jason may have been jealous. He was definitely jealous when Abby's niece and nephew were in town. They were 12 and 10 at that time. I was 25 and had a three-year-old. When the kids came to visit, I turned into a kid, again. I would play tag with them, run around the neighborhood after my daughter was in bed, play games and have a good time acting like a teenager. Abby was always telling my husband that I needed to let loose. She was right. I was bitter from not getting a full-time teaching job. I had a small child to take care of and a daycare full of kids in the basement. I had a lot going on. I needed to blow off steam. Back then, my way of blowing off steam was to be a kid again. I needed to release my frustrations with our daughter and with our relationship.

Jason was also jealous of my friendship with Abby because I spent more time with her and less time with him. Abby was easy to talk to; she listened and didn't judge. Abby made me feel like I mattered; she was always asking how I was doing and how my day was, and when I had a bad day, we would talk it through. I wasn't getting any of that from Jason. We rarely talked. He never asked how my day was. All we did was sit on the couch, watch T.V and eat junk food. He didn't support me in my dreams. He wanted me to get a teaching job so he could quit working. Jason did not help with disciplining Isobelle, making me feel like an awful parent when she would throw her tantrums and I couldn't control it. We were drifting apart, and we both knew it; we were headed for divorce. Neither one of us wanted to admit that our marriage was coming to an end, so we kept going.

● ● ●

Abby introduced me to tarot cards and pendulums. We would spend hours reading cards for each other and asking questions with the pendulum. She taught me how to read the cards and how to take care of them. I became obsessed with them. When Abby was at work, I took care of her dogs and spent time with the cards on my own. Sometimes I went over to her house three times a day to do a reading. The thing is, if you ask the same questions over and over, they stop being accurate. I didn't care; I wanted to read all the time. The cards gave me peace of mind about the questions I had. Questions about motherhood, marriage and life in general. I asked if I was doing a good job at motherhood a lot. Since my daughter has been a difficult child since two years of age, I wanted to know if I was doing the best I could or if I was a terrible mother. I had many relationship questions. I wanted to know if my marriage was over and if we were better off apart. I also wanted to know what I was meant to do with my life. The tarot cards answered my questions, not always the way I wanted, but it gave me clarity at the time. I didn't realize until now that I was addicted to the cards.

I bought my own set of tarot cards and a guidebook to learn how to do my own readings at home instead of sneaking over to Abby's house. I hid it from Jason, though. I didn't think he'd understand and that he would make fun of me. He wanted me to focus on finding a teaching job, but I was discouraged. I was pushing him away without realizing it. The only person who knew how much I loved tarot cards was Abby.

Abby and her partner always came to our house for dinner. Our daughter was about three at the time. We seemed to use the neighbors as a buffer so we didn't have to deal with our issues with parenting and communicating with each other. We never seemed to have a meal as a family with only the three of us. This went on for two years.

In the summer of 2006, I went to a few concerts with Abby. We met a band that we loved and talked to the musicians after each show. I got really close to the bassist. We'll call him Jack. He showed an interest in getting to know me. At one show, we exchanged numbers. We called each other almost every night to talk. I vented about my marriage and Isobelle. I felt like I couldn't talk to Jason because we would end up arguing about raising Isobelle or me still not getting a teaching job. But Jack listened, gave advice and made me feel better.

In August of 2006, Jason moved into the guest room. I could overhear him talking to a woman every night when I was in bed. I knew I had no right to be mad since I was talking to another man, but I was. He was dating her, but I wasn't dating the man I was talking to; he was my confidant, not a love interest, but I was emotionally cheating on Jason. It was then that we decided we needed a divorce.

I wanted to move out as soon as I could. I applied for low income housing and found a place that would be ready at the beginning of 2007. I moved out of our house and into a low-income townhome. It was a nice place, bad neighborhood, though. The house was only a few blocks from Jason, so it was easy to trade off weeks. I think that is how we started the schedule, anyway, every other week, or maybe I had her a bit more, I'm not sure. All I know is that I spent a lot of time alone in my house.

At the end of 2006, we both got lawyers and started the divorce process. Since I didn't want the house, nor could I afford it on my own, I let Jason have it with the stipulation that he pay me back for the money I put into it. I also asked for child support but didn't get it. His lawyer was a shark. Her reason for not giving me child support was because I didn't want the house and moved into low-income housing; therefore, I didn't need the extra support. The custody agreement was simple. I would have her for the school year, and Jason would take her in the summer. We switched off weekends.

Jason and I fought a lot during the divorce process, mainly over money. Jason was very adamant about not giving me child support or any other help. To this day, I am still trying to make ends meet. I am in charge of her cell phone bill, and I carry her on my health insurance, which is very expensive. I have Isobelle during the nine-month school year, so I am also responsible for her education. I felt and still feel overwhelmed and under-prepared.

The divorce was finalized in April of 2007. Isobelle was five. That was the first time I'd ever had to be alone. I had always had someone else living with me. To live alone was a new concept for me. After the divorce, we had to share custody of Isobelle, so every other weekend, it was just me.

I didn't have a teaching job, even though I graduated three years before that. I ended up working in a factory during the day and taught an after-school program in the afternoon. I was miserable. The fact that I still hadn't gotten a full-time teaching job was plenty, but to also have gone through a divorce was enough to put me over the edge. I felt like I had failed. I couldn't make my marriage work and had to work extra hard to support myself and my daughter. Teaching an after-school program was not what I went to school for. I wanted a full-time teaching job, not two part-time jobs that didn't pay enough to survive. I felt like my life had no purpose. I was going through the motions but not living. When I had my daughter, I would come home from work, make her dinner, play with her, bathe her, put her to bed and go to bed, myself. When I didn't have her, all I did was come home, make a few drinks, watch T.V and go to bed. When I went to concerts, I drank a lot and would have random hookups. I would always feel like shit in the morning from drinking too much and sleeping with some random guy. The random guys made me feel better at the time, but when it was over, I felt nothing. I had no idea what I wanted out of life or who I wanted to be.

PART 2
DOWNWARD SPIRAL

•••• 4 ••••

The Three D's: Drugs, Dudes and Drinking

You have to stop when you're lonely and listen.

—Charlotte Zolotow

STAYING IN SOUTHERN Minnesota after the divorce didn't help. I had no support system, few people that I considered friends and no family. That is not to say that the divorce was a bad thing. On the contrary, it was definitely a good thing. Jason and I were fighting too much, he had a girlfriend and I was just not in love with him, anymore.

I started going out a lot when I didn't have my daughter. I wanted to avoid the loneliness. That is when my band phase started. Abby and I would travel around to see Jack's band play as much as we could. It was another addiction for me. I had to see bands play every weekend. I would take my daughter to my mom's and leave to go see them play and get drunk. My priorities were watching live music and getting drunk instead of taking care of Isobelle.

My addiction to seeing bands was not healthy. That is all I wanted to do. Drinking goes hand in hand with bands and bars. Obviously, the bands I saw played at bars. Some people can go to a bar and not drink; I was not one of them. I needed the full experience of seeing the band and having the drinks. I used alcohol as an excuse to loosen up. The alcohol made me more social and outgoing. I talked more, danced, sang along with the music and had more fun than I did when I was sober.

Southern Minnesota had outdoor concerts in the summer, and I was always at them. I met a drummer at one of them, and we ended up hitting it off. Sort of. I knew the lead singer of his band, so he introduced us. We talked for an hour or so, then he invited me to snort coke with him and the guitarist. We found a spot under a bridge, downtown, and they both started to snort the coke. I wasn't sure about it, so I watched at first. I had never done coke, so I was scared. Ultimately, I decided that I wanted to try it. I wanted to know how it felt and what kind of high I would get. The first hit I took was weird; putting powder up my nose made me want to sneeze. I did another hit, and it felt better. After the third hit, I could feel my body relaxing and my head was getting foggy. I felt like I was on a cloud. It was such a rush. I hate to admit that, but it really was. I felt good, like I could do anything. A few more hits later, the drummer and I decided to go back to my place for a nightcap. We had a few drinks, some good conversation, at least I think it was good. Eventually, clothes came off, and we slept together. In the morning, we said goodbye. I only saw him at concerts after that. We never did get together again.

I only did coke one other time. I had a friend who could get some, so I took him up on it when he offered. We drove to the dealer's house, paid for our drugs and snorted a line in the car before leaving. My friend and I proceeded to snort the rest of the coke at his house. I was so high I didn't know my head from my ass. He kept trying to sleep with me, but I didn't want to. I knew he was angry about it, but I didn't care; I was not in the mood for it. All I wanted to do was snort more coke to see how high I could get. It made me feel like I was on top of the world and no one could hurt me. He could have taken advantage of me, but he didn't. He didn't like my decision, but he respected it. Thank God for that. I was putting myself in too many risky situations, and this time my brain kicked in to stop me from following through.

At the end of 2007, I met a singer/songwriter; we'll call him Mark. Mark caught my eye right away. He was on stage playing his guitar and singing. When he played, you could see how passionate he was; his eyes would close as he got deeper into the song. His voice is like a cross between Bob Dylan and Leonard Cohen. Mark is short, but he walks like he owns the world. He had the messiest hair I have ever seen; dark brown with blonde flecks; never combed, but so sexy the way it stuck up.

He knew how to make a girl feel special. We met after his show, and he blew everyone else off to talk to me. The show was a few hours away from my house, so my friend and I had a hotel room. Mark had his own room but ended up staying in ours because we spent the night talking and getting to know each other. Mark was so interested in my life and knowing everything about me. I don't even remember going to bed. In the morning as we said our goodbyes and exchanged phone numbers, he kissed me goodbye. Literally five minutes into my drive home, he texted me. My friend drove, annoyed, while Mark and I texted back and forth the whole way home.

Mark text me and called me every day. He liked to text me random song lyrics to see if I knew them. I would text back with the song it was from and then my own lyrics for him. When he called, we would talk about how our day was, our kids, music and movies. Sometimes, he would call in the middle of the night to either vent about his life or talk about random things. I looked forward to his calls because it made me feel needed. I would answer his call no matter what I was doing; even if it was the middle of the night and I was tired, I didn't care. I wanted to hear his voice.

We got together as much as we could to hang out. I usually went to his house for the weekend when my daughter was with her dad. He lived two hours away, so I always stayed with him for the whole weekend.

But Mark was an alcoholic and drug abuser: hard drugs and prescription drugs. He could be an angry drunk, but it was only when we were with other people that he would drink too much and get mean. When he had too much to drink, he yelled, drove off or threw things. He never physically hurt me, but it scared me. I would get upset and end up crying myself to sleep.

When we were alone, however, he didn't drink too much and was nice. When things were good, we had great times together. We would have a few drinks, talk and play guitar hero. We also talked non-stop and listened to music. I don't really remember what we talked about. I'm not even sure how we could talk so much and not run out of things to say. I loved being with him when it was only he and I. There were times we got together with our kids as well. We took the kids swimming a few times and to the Mall of America, and we never drank much with the kids around.

I had my second experience doing hard drugs with Mark. One night, we went to his dealer's house and smoked crack. Again, I hate to admit that I liked it, but I did. It made me feel alive, especially with Mark. I was flying high that night and into the next few days. He taught me how to smoke out of a crack pipe, rolling the pipe in my fingers while inhaling so I wouldn't burn my lips, holding the smoke in my lungs for as long as I could before exhaling. I felt calm, yet happy. I remember every moment of that weekend: the escort who told me never to leave my purse on the floor, that it was bad luck; the guy who was paranoid that the police were going to bust us; the game we played; thinking of as many dirty four-letter words as we could; lying on the couch with Mark as we fell asleep in each other's arms; smoking the rest of the crack at his house the next day. I felt very safe with him that weekend. He always made sure I was okay and that I never left his side.

Next came the prescription drugs. Vicodin and valium. We would take both and start nodding off. I remember him driving us back to his house after we both took some valium. He kept nodding off and swerving into traffic. I couldn't nod off because I was scared for my life. I made him pull over so I could drive the rest of the way. I was sleepy but alert enough to get home, probably because I was too afraid that I might die. That is one of the dumbest things I've done. First of all, neither of us was sober enough to drive, and second of all, we both had kids depending on us.

A few months had passed, and Mark and I decided it was time to move in together. Sort of. He was going on tour and needed someone to watch the house while he was away. I agreed, hoping we would grow closer. I began the process of trying to move away from Jason. I was still living in the townhouse only a few blocks from him, and when I told him that I wanted to move two hours away with our daughter, he was not thrilled; in fact, he took me back to court. The judge told Jason that he didn't care where I lived as long as it was still in Minnesota, so I changed my address, packed my things and off I went.

I never made it to Mark's house. At the last minute, he changed his mind, deciding to sell the house, instead. I felt like my whole world was crumbling. I was angry and hurt, actually, more like *crushed*. Can you imagine how stupid I felt? I uprooted my six-year-old daughter to move into Mark's house. I had to move into my parents' house until I could find a place of my own. Thank God for my wonderful mother. She is my angel. The worst part is, Mark never even went on tour. It fell through, and he rented his place out. Needless to say, after that, our romantic relationship was over.

After that, every now and then, he would contact me to hang out, and I always agreed to meet him wherever he was staying. He was trying to get sober, and I wanted to be there with him and for him. Plus, I wasn't ready to let him go. I went to a few AA meetings with him and met him for coffee when he needed to talk. That lasted for a year or two. Eventually, he stopped contacting me, and I had to let him go. We both moved on.

About five or so years later, I got a message from him on Facebook asking me about our time together. It was a step for AA. I told him how much he hurt me when he changed his mind about moving in. I told him how sad I would get whenever he'd get angry with me and leave. I let him know that he didn't force me to drink or do drugs with him; it was my choice. He apologized for hurting me and thanked me for being his friend. We are still friends on Facebook, but we haven't talked in several years. I think about him every now and then. I wonder how he is doing but don't have any unresolved feelings for him. I have let him go.

Before Mark and I were completely over and when I was still living in Southern Minnesota, I met another guy at a bar (we'll call him Dan). He was a singer. Go figure. We hit it off right away, although we were both drunk. Again, go figure. He came over to my house after the show and stayed the whole weekend. Isobelle was with her dad, so I was ok with him staying with me. We spent the weekend drinking and partying. We'd wake up in the morning and start drinking, again. We even went to a bar early Sunday morning. No one was there but us. He brought his guitar and played some songs at the bar. That was one of his bucket list items; to play his guitar in an empty bar for the bartender and the woman he was with, which happened to be me. We had a great time together and decided to keep in touch. He had to get home, so he went back to his apartment in Minneapolis. I saw him a few more times over the years. I would visit him when I was in town visiting my mom. I spent the weekend at his house a few times, and we always had to drink when we were together.

I need to rewind a bit to when Mark and I were still together. On New Year's Eve in 2007/2008, Mark and I got a hotel room in Minneapolis. He was opening for Prince's The Revolution band and invited me to come with. I was so excited to see The Revolution even if Prince wasn't there. I was also excited to see Mark on stage in such a cool venue.

As Mark drove us there, he held my hand the whole time. It felt good to have his hand in mine, like he really liked me and wanted to show it. We checked into a hotel room, dropped our stuff off and headed to the show. It was a short walk to the venue from the hotel. I was wearing a short skirt with high heels and a tight tank top so I was glad for the short walk. When we got there, we entered the VIP lounge and had some drinks with The Revolution and other bands that were playing. After a few drinks, it was time for Mark to take the stage. I can still picture the way he glided onto the stage with such ease and confidence. His hair was in his usual messy fashion and he was wearing a button down shirt and sexy jeans that made it look like he was a superstar. He started his set, and I was mesmerized. I couldn't take my eyes off of him. His voice was so unique, and he had this way of moving around the stage the made me melt.

After Mark's set, we listened to The Revolution for a little while and then went to a different bar for more drinks. Minneapolis is obviously very busy on New Year's Eve, so we ended up going back to the hotel bar to drink.

Mark and I were having a good time until we both had too much to drink. Mark was hitting on other girls, talking to everyone but me, and I was done with it. I called Dan. I told him what happened, and he walked over to the hotel, a few blocks from his apartment. We talked outside for a few minutes and then walked back to his place. We talked some more, I cried a bit and he hugged me. We started kissing. Dan and I had talked here and there since he had spent the weekend at my house, so it felt like we were picking up where we left off. He played some new songs he wrote, we made out some more and ended up having sex. We did have one more drink before he walked me back to my hotel. I was so drunk that I couldn't find my room. I knew it was upstairs, but that was about it. I wandered the halls for what felt like a million years until, finally, someone helped me find the correct room from my key. I walked in and Mark was back. When he looked at me, I could see in his eyes that he felt awful, and he apologized for being an asshole. I couldn't resist his charm. He got this look on his face like I was the only girl for him. He apologized a few more times with my hand in his, kissing the back of my hand. He kissed my cheek, my nose, my forehead, finally my lips. I had sex with him, too. Not one of my best decisions, considering I was drunk and upset, but I couldn't stop myself. I wanted to be with him.

This was when I moved from bad to worse regarding my relationships with men. For the next three years, I hopped into bed with different guys whenever I could. I was addicted to the attention I was getting. I met most of the guys at bars and a few at various places where I was working. The one common theme with all of the men was that they were all creative types, mostly musicians. There was a photographer, a writer and a boxer as well. I also met a few random men who just worked regular jobs, but they just didn't do it for me. I have always been more attracted to creative types.

I met one guy online. It was an awful experience. When he picked me up at my house, he wanted a tour, so I obliged. The first turn-off was that he didn't take his shoes off. I had brand-new carpet, and I hated when people didn't take off their shoes. We went to a restaurant for drinks and dinner, and he didn't open the door for me; he actually walked in first. We sat at the loud bar, and he barely talked to me. He was on his phone the whole time. To make matters worse, he made me pay. He looked at the check and then pushed it toward me. I looked at it, and I said, "do you want to go dutch or something?" He said, "I don't have money right now. I'll pay you back after I win at poker." I was dumbfounded; like, really dude? After dinner, he dropped me off with my friends because he had a poker tournament to attend. I was fine with that, and I spent the night at my friend's house. The guy had the nerve to text me at three a.m. asking for a booty call. I didn't respond.

Before I left Southern Minnesota, I did have one semi-serious relationship. We'll call him Dave. I had worked with Dave in a summer school program. We got to know each other while working with kids. We always had a good time at work, laughing and joking. Dave asked me out on a date, and I accepted. I don't remember where we went on our first date, but we dated for about nine months after that. He met my daughter, they got along really well, and I thought we were going to last. The problem was that he was a pothead. We fought a lot because he was always high and because I always wanted a drink. I was a total hypocrite. It was ok for me to have my vices, but not ok for others. Jason, my ex-husband, was also a pothead but quit for the most part when I was pregnant. So, when I saw Dave smoking all the time, it reminded me of when Jason used, and it bothered me. Dave and I didn't agree on many things, and eventually we decided to call it quits. When we finally did break up, I was sad; I knew it was not a good relationship, but it still hurt and it just added to my sadness and loneliness.

There are several more stories about one-night stands and stupid decisions. I kept a list of all of the men I had slept with over the years, mainly because my memories were all running together. It was hard to keep track; a lot of the stories seemed to overlap in my mind. My list kept growing, and I got more and more depressed as time went on.

Jason once told me that I was probably meant to be alone and that my mom agreed. He said that because I was dating different men but never settling down with any of them. I believed him. I thought there was something wrong with me. I know my own mother would never say that about me, though, but the thought stung just the same. He wanted to drive the knife in further, make me hurt more than I already did. I already felt like a failure; so, was he trying to push me over the edge, or was he just hurting as badly as I was?

All these men had something in common, though. They all had addictions. I was drawn to men with addictions for some reason. Was it because I thought I could help them, or was it because I was feeding my own addictions? I was addicted to addictions. I was addicted to suffering. I had chosen unavailable men to be with. I knew they weren't good for me, but I didn't care. It was like I wanted to feel the pain because it was better than feeling nothing at all.

Have you ever heard the saying that what you don't like in others is a reflection of yourself? I believe that to be very true. I was using other people's addictions to mask my own. The fear of facing my own demons was too strong; I wasn't showing up as my best self as a mother, as a daughter, as a friend. I wanted to help others with addictions, but I needed to help myself first.

·····5·····

Despair

Isolation is like a tomb.

—Ian Kennedy Martin

SOMETIMES, WHEN YOU are alone for too long, it can feel like you are in trapped in a small, dark space fighting to survive. I have felt that way too many times to count. It is a terrible feeling when you've been drinking alone, and no one will answer their phone.

Not only did I drink too much, sleep around and experiment with drugs, but I was also very down. I managed to make it through a workday just fine, although I did job hop a bit. I worked in a factory, did after-school care, did summer care for school kids and finally got a job as a paraprofessional for a 2nd grader. The only reason I could make it through a workday was because I had a child of my own to support, and I also had my school kids who depended on me. I was strong in that way, at least. Believe me, there were many days when I wanted to stay in bed. And I probably would have stayed in bed if it wasn't for my daughter. She needed me.

Isobelle wasn't there when I drank too much or went out, but even when she was home, I still had a hard time getting out of bed. I wanted to sleep the day away. Isobelle didn't let me do that. She wanted to play and have fun. I forced myself to get out of bed and take care of her. I forced myself to have fun with her. She deserved that. I would take Isobelle to the park on nice days, go to the mall park on rainy days or watch movies. We played games and played with her toys. I did love doing those things. Spending time with her made me feel better, and seeing her smile put a smile on my own face.

Although we did have a hard relationship at times, and still do, Isobelle and I always made our relationship work. Isobelle likes to argue and get her way. When she was little, when she didn't get her way, she would throw fits. Really bad fits. She would scream and cry until I'd have to give in for fear of getting the cops called on me. When she would scream, it would be loud and ear piercing. I would worry that if someone heard it, they would probably think I was hurting her, so I would give in; that was better than people thinking I abused my kid. Isobelle still has screaming fits to this day, but she can control them more, and she finally feels bad when she yells at me.

Even though Isobelle and I had our fair share of rough days, the sadness I felt when she was with her dad was always bad. When Isobelle was gone, I had no one who needed me. What was the point of getting out of bed? Getting ready for the day? What was the point of going on if no one needed me?

When I couldn't find something to do or someone to hang out with, I spent my time alone in my house. I drank a lot, which made me more sad. I wrote depressing poetry and drank even more. I never wanted to ask for help or tell anyone what I was going through. Maybe I was embarrassed or maybe I didn't think I had a problem. It was probably both.

I barely ate, so I lost a lot of weight. I thought that was a good thing, but since I drank on an empty stomach, I got drunk much faster and had bad hangovers. On the weekends, I would stay in my pajamas all day and watch TV I'd start drinking in the early afternoons, sometimes even in the mornings. I texted friends to see if they wanted to go out. Sometimes, I was able to find something to do. It was when I couldn't find anything to do that things got bad.

I would sit alone for long periods of time, thinking about how shitty my life had gotten. I'd pour myself another drink and drown out the noise in my head, waiting by my phone, hoping someone would call until I gave up and either passed out or just went to bed. I also smoked a lot. I liked to go outside, light a cigarette, smoke it to the filter and put it out on my skin. I wanted to feel the pain. I wanted to feel something, anything. I held the burning cigarettes to my arms, hands and legs, watching them eat my flesh and form ashy blisters on my skin. When I would wake up the next day and see what I had done, my first thought would be, *what the hell did I do to myself?* My demons were taking over my body, making me do terrible things. I wanted to feel physical pain. I could pinpoint where the pain was coming from. But you can't pinpoint emotional pain, it's all over. In your head. In your heart. In your soul. And injuring myself made me feel alive.

It went on like this week after week. The same routine over and over. Then one day, I decided enough was enough, and after drinking my last drink for the night, I chased it with a bottle of pills. I took pill after pill, dropping some on the floor, scrambling to pick them up so I wouldn't miss one. I prayed before passing out that I wouldn't wake up. I wanted the pain to stop. I wanted to leave this world. I thought that I was ready to give up.

I knew that the pills I took wouldn't kill me, they weren't strong enough. I was hoping that they would, but deep down I didn't want to die. I wanted the *pain* to die. The only thing that happened when I woke up was that I had a killer headache and more pain. The fact that God didn't take me was all I could think about. Why didn't he listen? I asked him to make the pain go away. I asked him to take me out of this life. My life was worthless. I couldn't do anything right. Why didn't God take me home?

The next time I was alone, I tried again, only this time with stronger pills and more of them. I prayed even harder this time, but God still didn't listen. I woke up with a bigger headache and stomachache. To cure that, I decided to have a drink. It helped the physical pain but did nothing for the emotional pain.

My only escape from the cycle was going to my mom's house with my daughter every other weekend. I knew I wouldn't try to hurt myself there, not with Isobelle or my mom around. They were my saviors for those weekends. My mom knew something wasn't right with me, though. She suggested I go to the doctor. I don't like disappointing my mom, so I went. I knew I was sad; I knew I had a problem, but who wants to admit that? It was a big step to tell the doctor how I was really feeling. But I wasn't going for me; I was going for my mom and Isobelle, so that step was a little easier to take because of that. I did the depression questionnaire, and I was clinically diagnosed with depression.

I was put on antidepressants and got hooked up with a therapist. I went to counseling once and hated it. I couldn't sit there and talk about my feelings with a stranger, so I quit going. But I stayed on the antidepressants. I needed to take them in order to get healthy.

I was told not to mix alcohol with the antidepressants. Apparently, if you mix the two, it can make depression worse. Besides that, suicidal thoughts are a side effect of the medication. Suicidal thoughts from a pill that is supposed to make me happy sounded strange to me. Shit, I *already had* suicidal thoughts. But I'm not a doctor, so I took them. I stopped drinking, too. Things were getting better. My mood was up, and I was feeling happier. They were working. For now.

Now that I had medication to help me, I figured I could have a drink every now and then, too. I told myself that I'd be fine. I didn't have any suicidal thoughts; I was happy, so what could it hurt? As it turned out, it can hurt a lot.

I had my first drink while on the medication a few months after I was on it. I was home alone that weekend and decided to pour myself a drink. One drink turned into two and two turned into five and so on. The only thing that happened that first time was that I got drunk a lot faster. I still felt fine otherwise. I thought, maybe I was one of the few that could take antidepressants and still drink.

I continued to do that on the weekends at first, and then I'd have a few beers after work sometimes. No big deal. Every now and then I'd have too many and have to go to work hung-over. It sucked, but I never missed work for it. I remained responsible in that way. How could I have a problem if I was still going to work and taking care of my kid?

Then one weekend something shifted. I found myself alone and feeling down. I already had a few drinks and took my meds. I figured it would pass; it was just a bad day. The sadness must have been slowly creeping back in without me being aware of it. I was sitting on the couch that night, crying and writing in a journal about wanting to die. I have no idea where it came from. It's like the sadness took over my brain, and I couldn't stop it. I went into the kitchen, found my meds and downed the bottle with the last gulp of my drink. I knew that wouldn't work, so I got the sharpest knife I could find out of the drawer. My hands were shaking, and I was terrified. I put the knife to my wrist, found my vein, pressed down as hard as I could and started cutting through the skin.

It hurt like hell. Blood started flowing from my wrist. When I saw the blood, I dropped the knife to the floor. I fell to my knees and cried. It felt like hours had passed, but it was only minutes. I opened my eyes, picked up the knife and started on the other wrist. It took so long to break the skin this time, using my bloody left hand was hard. I managed to break through; the cut was much deeper than my left wrist. And as the blood was dripping from my wrists, I laid my face on the cool kitchen floor and closed my eyes.

I woke up the next morning in a daze. I didn't know where I was. My head was spinning, and I felt like I was going to throw up. I laid there for a long time, willing myself to feel better, cursing God for not taking me, crying. When I finally had the courage to sit up, I saw what I had done. Dried blood all over the floor, on my hands, fresh wounds on my wrists covered in dried blood, an empty pill bottle on the floor and an empty bottle of vodka on the counter.

How could I still be alive? I couldn't for the life of me think of why God wanted me to live. For my daughter? For my mom? Did I have unfinished business?

I sat there on my kitchen floor in shock for what felt like a lifetime. I eventually picked myself up off the floor and cleaned up the kitchen, took a shower and bandaged my wrists. After I cleaned myself up, I sat on the couch and watched movies for the rest of the weekend, fading in and out of sleep. I went nowhere. I talked to no one. I was ashamed, embarrassed, but most of all—I wanted out. Out of this life, out of the overwhelming sadness, just out.

I went to work the following Monday as if nothing had happened. I didn't speak of that night to anyone until right now, as I write this. My daughter was only six at the time, but she saw the bandages on my wrists and asked what happened. I told her I burned myself taking pizza out of the oven. She told her dad about it, and he asked me about it. I lied and told him the same story. He knew better and told me that If

I need to talk, he was there. I never took him up on that offer. Why would I? We were divorced, and I wasn't his problem to solve. Besides, he was the one who said I was meant to be alone.

I know now that he was not only concerned for me but also concerned for our daughter. He had every right to be concerned. I screwed up big-time, and I felt awful. What was I thinking? Why would I leave my daughter without a mom at such a young age? She was only 6. How would she feel, knowing her mother committed suicide?

That's the thing about depression. I wasn't thinking about how my actions would affect others, I was only thinking about how sad I was and how I didn't belong in this world. Depression is a demon that took over my mind and body, it controlled my thoughts and it controlled my actions.

After that horrible night, I vowed to take my meds appropriately and not drink while I was on them. I also decided that it was time to move back home. I needed to be closer to my mom. I didn't want to be alone, anymore. I wanted to get better.

Before I moved, I ordered a bottle of valium from some internet site based in China. One of my friends from work who I had confided in told me that it helped him relax when he took it with antidepressants, so I figured that it would help me relax and was worth a shot.

Abusing unprescribed valium and alcohol to numb my pain to escape my life was not a good idea. I ordered valium online so I didn't have to see a doctor. I liked the feeling that valium gave me. When I took it, I felt numb, I had no pain. I was not learning how to feel or work through my feelings; all I did was learn how to make myself numb. I had to learn to let my feelings in, process them. In the 12-step program, it says to create a self-inventory of all your wrongdoings and make amends for them. Of the 12 steps, this was the only step I did because it strongly resonated with me. Writing down the things I was ashamed of helped me to overcome the guilt, one of the strongest emotions I was running from. I wrote things down and then burned them, let my shame go up in smoke after I made amends to the people I had wronged, including myself. I was really good at hurting myself, so for me, it was mostly myself I was making amends to.

Early 2007 to late 2009 was the toughest time in my life. From being depressed and drinking too much to using drugs occasionally and sleeping around, I was headed down a terrible road. I got so good at hiding my pain that no one really knew how bad it was. I liked it that way. Anyone who suffers from depression and addiction knows how hard it is to seek help or even admit that you have a problem. I didn't want to talk to anyone about it; I could get through it on my own, or so I thought.

····6····
Settling Down

Looking for happiness is like clutching a shadow or chasing the wind.

—Japanese Proverb

I WAS LOOKING for happiness in all the wrong places. Happiness isn't something to be found. Happiness is always present, you just have to experience it by living in the now and being grateful for what you have.

Although I wasn't able to find happiness in all the places I was looking so far, I thought I could start by finding a new place to live. I searched for several months and finally found an apartment a few blocks from my mom's house. I needed my own place, but I still needed my mom close. She is my rock. Life was still hard; I hadn't found a good teaching job, yet, wasn't making enough money to make ends meet and still needed to rely on meds and sometimes alcohol to make me feel better. I was working several jobs to stay afloat, none of which I truly loved.

I met a man online in December of 2009. We'll call him Kevin. A few months into dating, he decided to move into my apartment building a floor down from mine. We figured that, eventually, Isobelle and I would move into his apartment. Kevin helped with my rent until my lease was up, which was six months. Isobelle and I ended up moving in with him three months before my lease expired, and we sublet my apartment to his brother for the remaining months.

We drank a lot together. He could never do anything without alcohol. We had our cocktails every night, and he usually had more than me. He had a habit of staying up late, drinking and talking really loud on the phone. There were a lot of occasions I had to tell him to quit talking so loudly and to go to bed. We argued a lot about that. He didn't see a problem with how loud he was and woke Isobelle up a few times. I would ask him to keep it down when Isobelle and I went to bed, but it never got any better.

There were so many warning signs over the course of the relationship. He would skip out on work because of aches and pains. He got irritated when I spent time with my mom. He hated when I had to drive an hour to drop my daughter off with her dad. He was always lying about how much money he brought in. He spent too much money, didn't pay taxes and I had to cosign on a motorcycle loan for him. I caught him texting—or should I say, *sexting*—other women, and he drank way too much.

I let all those things slide because I couldn't handle being alone, again. I knew the relationship wasn't good for me, but I couldn't help it. I thought I could change him, or help him. But you can't change someone who doesn't want to change.

I realize now that it was a very toxic relationship, to say the least. I should have seen the big red flag flying in front of my face. I didn't want to be alone, though, so I stayed, and

I mistook this false sense of security as happiness. But the longer I stayed, the worse things got.

We both made mistakes. He got a DUI and lost his license while I was with my cousins for a girl's weekend. I was not happy. It caused a lot of headaches and extra work for me. Because he couldn't drive, I ended up driving him all the way to Missouri and back when his grandpa died. A few months later, he was out with his friends, and I was out with mine; I drank too much, and the girls told me not to drive, but I did, anyway. I ended up in Minneapolis, which is the wrong way from where I lived. I don't know how I ended up there. I remember opening my eyes while I was still driving, seeing where I was, and freaking out. I drove the rest of the way home in a panic. I had to pee so bad, but I wanted to get home and crawl into bed, so I didn't stop and pissed my pants. Yup, one of my most shameful moments. It was horrible; I felt so stupid and was so ashamed of myself. I'm surprised I didn't get pulled over and end up with a DUI myself or worse, kill someone. But I made it home in *almost* one piece, with everything but my dignity. After that night, I didn't get down on Kevin for his DUI anymore. It was a mistake he made, and he paid for it. And I paid for mine through my shame.

It wasn't all bad, and there were good times. I did fall in love with him, at least I thought I did. I think I was more in love with the idea of being in love. We had fun together, yet, the good times we shared were always shared with alcohol. We both had to have a drink in order to have fun, even when we were just watching a movie together. The drinking was my way out of a bad relationship; instead of leaving, I numbed the emotional pain with a drink. That way, I didn't have to focus on how bad the relationship was.

I know Kevin loved Isobelle. He played games with her and enjoyed spending time with her for the most part. Although he did get annoyed with her a lot. As I've said, Isobelle has a very strong personality and is always right, which made their relationship hard. Kevin would try to discipline Isobelle, but she wouldn't listen; they both whined to me about each other. I was in a tough spot to be in.

Two years into our relationship, Kevin decided to go to North Dakota for work. He said he was going to make a lot of money for us. He had family in North Dakota that he could stay with. He was supposed to get a job on the oil rigs, work a few weeks at a time, then come home for a week.

I have to back up a little. Kevin was a hypochondriac. There was always something wrong with him. He had headaches, back pain, sore feet, you name it, he had it all. He loved telling everyone about his woes. When he cut his finger, he called everyone he knew to talk about it. I heard the story at least fifty times. I got so sick of hearing about his aches and pains that I stopped listening. I pretended I was listening, made the faces, responded in one syllable words. He didn't realize I wasn't listening. He was too self-involved to notice.

When he got to North Dakota, he saw what the job entailed and backed out. He claimed his back couldn't handle it, and he'd probably end up dead. He took a job for fifteen bucks an hour, instead. He could have done that in Minnesota. Needless to say, I ended up paying most of the rent and bills for him. I had to borrow money from my mom, *again*. It was awful. I wasn't in a good financial place to carry most of the rent and bills.

He was gone for about six months, and during that time, he could only afford to come home once about two months after he left. Our relationship was strained by then. I was resentful, and my heart wasn't with him anymore.

The first month he was gone we talked on the phone all the time. But about a week after he got there, he told me that he wasn't going to work on the oil rigs. I realized then that I didn't want to be with him anymore since he wasn't doing what he set out to do. I started living my life as if I didn't even have a boyfriend. I barely called him, didn't text him, didn't even think about him much. I went to work, took care of Isobelle and went out with friends sometimes.

The one time he could afford to visit I was already fed up and ready to move on. I didn't even care that he came to visit. After he went back to North Dakota, I started the process of looking for somewhere else to live. One night we were talking on the phone, and I told him I was done and not more than an hour later, he was on his way back. It didn't matter, though, I was already checked out. It was over.

When Kevin got back, he stayed in the spare room. Kevin kept trying to fix our relationship by telling me that he was going to get a better job, pay his taxes and not drink so much. I didn't want to wait for that. I didn't believe him. I didn't believe him because he had a bottle of whiskey in his room and he wasn't looking for a job. I told him I couldn't be with him and that it was over.

I decided to move back into my mom's house until I found a place of my own. I was alone, living with my mom— *again*. I wasn't taking my meds anymore because I thought I was happy. Wrong. Depression reared its ugly head, *again*. I was lonely. I wanted this time to be different. I didn't want to drown in it. I wanted to find real happiness, but I didn't. I dated a few men, slept around some more, continuing to numb my depression with men. I did that for a few months, and then I met Aaron.

Aaron was amazing. I know, so was Kevin and Mark and every other guy I dated more than once. I met Aaron online, too. We talked for a week on the phone before we met in person. We seemed to have a lot in common, so we met for drinks. We talked all night, shut the bar down and went back to his house to watch a movie. We both fell asleep on the couch. I went home the next morning, and we texted each other all day. We went out on a few more dates, and then decided it was time for us to get our kids together. The girls all got along really well that day until it was time to leave the

Mall of America. We were supposed to spend the night at Aaron's house but Isobelle didn't want to stay the night and ended up having a meltdown on the way to his house. Aaron handled it really well. He didn't freak out about her fit; he let me handle it while trying to comfort me as Isobelle was screaming and yelling. I got her to calm down, and we ended up having a good time at his house with all three girls.

Aaron and I only dated for two months before I moved into his house. We moved fast because I was living with my mom. I wanted to move out of my mom's before school started for Isobelle. I made that decision without even thinking about it. I didn't think about how it would affect Isobelle. I only thought about myself and my own happiness. Isobelle didn't take the move very well. She was extremely mad at me; yelling, crying and threatening to move to her dad's. She eventually calmed down and moved with me even though she didn't want to.

There were only two bedrooms in the house, so all three girls had to share a room at first. That only lasted for a week. It was too cramped when they were all there together. Aaron and I moved our room downstairs and moved Isobelle into the master bedroom. Isobelle was much happier with her own room.

We had the girls together every other weekend, so we were always trying to find things for them to do. Aaron raced cars, so we went to the racetrack a lot. We also went to Wisconsin Dells two summers in a row for a week at a time. Aaron's two girls; Darla and Sophie, are younger than Isobelle. Isobelle and Darla didn't get along very well. They always argued and fought, and Darla would cry when she couldn't do what Isobelle did. Darla was always jealous that Isobelle got to bring a friend on our trips to the Dells. We let Isobelle bring a friend because she was twelve and they could go into the waterpark at our hotel without our supervision. It made for tough vacations, but we made the most of it. Aaron and I tried to make our trips fun for all the girls, even the small trips to the racetrack or to the Mall of America.

A year into the relationship, Aaron asked me to marry him, and I said yes. I thought we were happy and meant to be together. I found my forever. I found the person to spend my life with, the person who wanted to be with me and support me with my dreams. Aaron wanted to get married right away, but I wanted to wait because I was looking into changing my career. So, we decided to wait for a year.

I *did* decide to change my career. I wasn't going anywhere with teaching. I needed a change, and I found a school for massage therapy. I have no idea where the idea came from. I think it fell into my lap from heaven. Aaron supported me 100%. I was excited and scared but ready for the change. I was happy to make a big change and happier to have Aaron support me while I made it.

I loved going back to school. I took four to five classes each semester so I was able to graduate in 18 months. Some of the classes were tough, but I made it through. The actual massage classes were fun. We got to practice on each other as well as volunteer clients. Learning massage was not only a way to make money but also a healing journey. Before I graduated, I was able to start working as a massage therapist while still taking classes. I worked at Massage Envy. It was a great job, and I loved it. I met so many wonderful people and was able to help them heal physically and emotionally. I also met awesome co-workers. I thought I had found my calling.

With me back in school, there was a lot of stress in the house. We were both trying to be good step-parents as well parent our own kids. It was a hard road. Captain Morgan was a good friend in that relationship. We usually had two or three drinks a night during the week and more on weekends. The alcohol was a stress reliever for both of us. The girls were struggling to get along since they are all strong-willed and like their own ways, and I was focused more on school than anything else. It made for a tough living situation. Aaron liked things a certain way, and my daughter didn't follow his rules very often. I can't blame her; she was used to my rules. And I didn't have many. It's hard to have rules when your kid has a temper. I didn't like to wake the beast. Because of this, Isobelle and Aaron had a bad relationship. He got frustrated when she didn't listen, she got frustrated when he made her do things she didn't want to do. They argued a lot, and when his girls were around, he either ignored Isobelle or yelled at her.

Our relationship was slowly falling apart. I knew in my heart it wasn't going to last, but I kept pushing on, hoping it would work itself out. There was a lot of strain from me going to school. I was always doing homework or going to class, so Aaron had to watch the kids a lot. He had to take care of my daughter when I had night classes. I found out that he would sit in the basement and watch TV while my daughter was upstairs by herself. That pissed me off. They didn't have a great relationship as it was, so you'd think he would have tried harder to make the relationship better by spending time with her. I thought if they spent time together it would get better. Clearly that wasn't the case.

I thought this relationship was going to work. We were going to get married and have a life together. I was kidding myself. A year after his proposal, he broke it off. I wasn't even out of school yet; he supported me in my decision to go to school, and all of a sudden I lost his support. I came home from work one night, and he was waiting for me outside with a bag packed. I was completely blindsided. He told me it was over and that I had to move out in two weeks. He didn't even explain why; he just wanted me gone. He told me he was going to stay with his friend until I was moved out.

I was devastated. I had a feeling it was coming, but it hit me like a ton of bricks. I sobbed all night. I didn't know what to do. I made my daughter move to a new town, transfer to a different school and live with two other kids. I did this all to be with a man who broke my heart. I felt stupid and more alone than ever. The good thing was, my daughter was spending the summer with her dad, so she didn't have to see me so upset.

I was so distraught the next day that I had to miss work for the first time in years. I am a very proud person, and skipping out on a job is not in my nature. My eyes were swollen, my head was throbbing and my spirit was gone. I couldn't focus on healing others if I couldn't heal myself. My boss understood completely; she was very kind about it.

The first thing I did was call my mom. She was very supportive and understanding. She wanted me to move back in with her until an apartment became available, again. It was August, and school was going to start in less than a month. I spent the day changing my address, transferring schools for Isobelle, getting a storage unit and packing. I had a lot to do, and I kept myself busy so I wouldn't be sad.

I had to tell Isobelle the news, and I was terrified. I thought she would be so angry, having to go to a different school *again*. To my surprise, she was happy. She couldn't wait to get back to Rogers. She hated living with Aaron and hated the town. It was a blessing in disguise.

When my friends at work found out what happened, they were so amazing about it. Two of my fellow massage therapist friends showed up at my house the night after the breakup to help me pack and visit. They brought cupcakes and old dishes from Goodwill. Those women were incredible. I have never had such wonderful friends. We talked, laughed, ate cupcakes, shamed Aaron and had a good time. I know, shaming someone isn't great, but it felt good at the time.

The sun went down, and it was dark, except for the light of the moon. My friends had bought the plates and glasses from Goodwill for a therapeutic purpose. We each had a plate and a glass. We walked out to the driveway to a small section that no one parked in. I held up the plate and threw it as hard as I could onto the blacktop. We took turns smashing the plates and glasses until they were gone. Taking my anger out on dishes felt so good. The rush of adrenaline I got was indescribable. It was an awesome night. Breaking things was a good way to release my anger. If you ever feel so angry and sad at the same time, buy some old shit from Goodwill and smash it.

After I cleaned up the broken glass of our smashing party, it got quiet, again. I had to spend a few nights alone in that house, and it was awful. I cried a lot, didn't eat much and took a lot of naps. I found myself spiraling into depression, again. I had the added weight of having to move my life one more time because of another failed relationship.

I didn't post a lot of things on Facebook, but I needed help. I needed to move as quickly as possible because I couldn't spend one more night in that house, so I posted that I needed help moving. An old friend from high school responded. With the help of him, his wife and my parents, I was able to move all of my things out in a couple of days. I hadn't seen this man in years, but he was willing to help, no questions asked. I can't tell you how grateful I was that I had such wonderful people in my life.

An apartment became available a few short months after moving back to my mom's. It was in the same place I had lived before, so it was familiar and convenient. I liked living close to my mom, again. I loved my job and my friends, but Aaron's house was old and dingy and too small and the town isn't very nice, so I didn't miss that. That made it a little easier to move on.

A few weeks had passed, and I wanted to know why Aaron suddenly wanted to split. I was still angry and hurt, but I had to know his reason. He agreed to talk, so I met him at his house. We sat outside on the front steps and looked at each other for a long time before speaking. Eventually, he told me that he couldn't handle my kid. She was too much for him. I was surprised by his response. He knew that my daughter was headstrong and had a temper before we moved in together. He knew she was difficult, yet he invited us into his life, anyway. He asked me to marry him for God's sake. I couldn't say anything; all I could do was stare at him, mouth hanging open. I felt the tears welling up in my eyes and had to look away. When I finally found my words, all I said was "wow." I had no other words. I got up, said goodbye and left. His reason didn't sit right with me, but I let it go. I found out later that he had met someone new. I don't remember how I found out, but I did. My instinct that there was more to the story was right. I'm still not sure why he couldn't man up and tell me that he had met someone else.

The thing that really broke my heart was that he didn't let me say goodbye to his kids. I had grown close to them. I asked him if I could see them before I left the house, but he refused. He said it would be too hard on them. I hated not being able to say goodbye to the girls. They were in my life for nearly two years, and it felt terrible to not see them one more time, hug them one more time, kiss their heads one more time.

● ● ●

I started dating one of my mom's neighbors about a year after Aaron and I broke up. We'll call him Trevor. We had a pretty good relationship. We went to dinner a lot, went to car shows and concerts and had fires with the neighbors. We also sat around talking and watching mindless television. Trevor had two kids: a boy and a girl. Lexi is the same age as Isobelle, and they went to the same school. They weren't really friends, but when we got together with the kids, both Lexi and Isobelle got along fine. Isobelle really liked Trevor; they had and still have a great relationship.

I think my drinking got in the way, though. I remember going to some carnival thing in the park by my apartment. I filled a travel mug with my captain coke mix and brought it with me, and he called me out on it. He said I shouldn't need to have a drink to go to a kid's carnival. And he was right. I knew it was stupid, and I understood his concerns.

After almost a year of dating, we broke up. We decided that neither one of us was ready for a serious relationship. At least, that is what I remember about the situation, anyway. We tried to date again a few months or so after we initially broke up, but my heart wasn't in it, anymore. I don't think his was, either. We are still good friends, though; we hang out at our weekly fires during the summer and still have fun. He is always very supportive of my passion for writing. I am blessed to have him as my friend.

After we broke up, I decided to be single. I had a few one-night stands here and there, but nothing big. It took a while to be ok with being alone, but once I got used to it, I loved it. I got so used to being single, I didn't think I could handle being in a relationship, again. I was enjoying my time to myself. I discovered that am actually an introvert, meaning I recharge by being alone. Given my history of filling empty spaces of myself with relationships with men, this was a very unexpected discovery for me. But once I understood this about myself, I started to use my time alone to get to know myself and to recharge my batteries by focusing on what makes me happy.

I was single for about three years, give or take. In April of 2019, after starting this book, I got a Facebook message from an old friend. It was my very first boyfriend, Travis, the one my mom didn't like. He wanted to know how I was doing and also wanted to thank me for the time I gave him a ride when he was in a bind. We messaged back and forth and talked on the phone for two weeks getting to know each other again. We finally went out on a date two weeks after our initial conversation and couldn't stop talking while we ate. It was so much fun getting to know him as an adult.

It has now been over two months since we have reconnected, and I couldn't be happier. We spend a lot of time together talking and laughing. We have so much in common it's almost scary. Being in a new relationship is nice, yet I am still ok with myself and being alone. Being in this kind of headspace gives me the freedom to enjoy the relationship while still having time for myself and my own needs. This relationship did not work out. I was sad but I know what I want and that wasn't it.

PART 3
GETTING BY

••••7••••

Moving Around

The things we take with us when we die will nearly all be small things.

—Storm Jameson

IN 2014, I was still living in the apartments. I didn't know any of my neighbors, and I didn't make an effort to get to know anyone. Each day, I came home, threw on my pajamas, poured myself a drink, made dinner and went to bed. That was my routine. Every day. When my daughter was home, I spent time with her watching our shows or movies, talking or playing games.

Life went on like that for almost three years. I took a lot of online classes, hoping to find a career I truly loved. Nothing ever came out of the classes. I learned a lot, but I couldn't seem to start a business of my own. I had so many ideas and plans for my life. When none of them panned out,

I decided to just quit. I took a factory job and stopped trying to better my life. I lost all hope that I could do what I love and live a comfortable life with my daughter. I had to work my ass off to make ends meet because that's the way life is for the middle/lower class. I had to accept it. It's what I was taught. Work your ass off, pay your bills, retire in your late sixties, die. But I didn't accept that. That is not what life should be like. I wanted something better. I deserved something better.

In 2017, my mom retired. She and my dad wanted to move to Arizona but didn't want to sell the Minnesota house. My mom asked me to move into the house and take care of it. She also wanted to be able to come visit for extended trips and not stay at a hotel. It was a win-win situation. I got to leave the over-priced apartments, move into a house that I love and have neighbors that are already great friends. My mom got to move to Arizona but keep her house in Minnesota knowing that I would take care of it.

I was excited to move. I finally had somewhere that felt like home to me and my daughter. It was hard to live there when my parents were visiting, I should say, when my dad came with. My mom by herself was good. My mom and I would sit and watch the television show Friends, talk, laugh and reminisce. We would also get pedicures and go to lunch. When my dad came, there was arguing and fighting. My dad argued with my daughter the most. I tried to keep my mouth shut, but sometimes it was really hard. He's another one who is always right about everything. He also has a very short fuse with a big temper. Living there was still a good situation for my daughter and me, regardless of the arguing when my dad was here. I wouldn't change it for the world.

I liked to have drinks when my mom visited; partly because my dad stresses me out and partly because I liked to have a drink or two with my mom. I didn't feel out of control when I drank with my mom. Sometimes, I would have too much when we were out at a fire and wake up with a hangover, but I didn't get depressed or drink to numb myself. I had fun. When they went back to Arizona, I didn't drink at all. I didn't even keep any alcohol in the house. I've noticed that if I have alcohol in the house, I will drink it. When there is no alcohol, I don't miss it and I don't have the urge to go buy it.

• • •

From 2009 to 2014 I had moved seven times. That is way too many times to be moving, especially with a child. I felt bad for moving my daughter so many times. I can't imagine how she felt. I was so concerned with my own unhappiness that I didn't think about how it would affect her. Changing homes and schools had to be hard for her. I still feel bad to this day for moving her around so much.

Isobelle seems to be growing up perfectly fine despite my messed up decisions with men and moving her around. She is a strong, smart young woman, although still very headstrong. We don't always get along; she is a know-it-all teenager. In fact, we still argue, just not as much, and there are times I would really like to smack some sense into her. But I love when she talks to me and confides in me. And I admire how Isobelle doesn't hold anything back. The girl has the biggest potty mouth I have ever heard, and I love it.

Despite feeling bad for moving Isobelle and the circumstances involved; I am actually happy to have made all the moves. With each move I made, I got rid of stuff I didn't need or didn't use. It also made the next move easier: less crap. It also felt good to get rid of things. I really hate clutter. I have learned that home is where I make it. I feel at home in my mom's house, but I am looking forward to what the future holds.

····8····

Jobs, Jobs, Jobs

Out of difficulties grow miracles.

—Jean De La Bruyere

MY DAD WAS always looking for work when I was growing up. He never had a steady job, which left my mom as the breadwinner. She always had two or three jobs while my brother and I were in school. My brother and I both got jobs at sixteen years old so we could buy our own things. Even at that age, I didn't want to ask my mom for money, anymore. She worked really hard to give my brother and I a good life. It was my turn to earn my own money.

I worked at McDonald's for four years; it was my first job. That is probably the longest job I've ever had. Although I am never without a job, after a few years at the same one, I get restless and I'm ready to move on. I believe I get that from my dad. He quit jobs because he didn't get along with the people. Sometimes he'd get fired because he's a know-it-all and wants to change things on day one. That is not me. I get bored doing the same thing, and I like change. Maybe it's not great to change jobs all the time, but I have never been happy staying in one place, especially the places I was working. I'm thinking that this is probably because I have never been passionate about any of the jobs I've had in my whole life.

When I was a teacher, or trying to be one, I went from school to school trying to get my foot in the door. It never worked. I was denied for many reasons: I didn't have enough experience; I was too good as a substitute teacher; they needed me as a paraprofessional; I even got rejected because I'm a woman. The last one hit me hard. They justified it by saying they needed more male teachers in that particular school. I was more qualified and had more experience than any of the other applicants, and the man they hired was fresh out of school. The job was for a teaching role with the students I had been working with in an after-school program for two years. I knew all of the ins and outs of the class. It made me feel overlooked when they picked someone who didn't have any experience. It was a kick in the face.

I started working with a homebound student in 2010. I was teaching basic skills for 10 hours a week, working as a PCA for the same kid 20 hours a week, cleaning their house 10 hours a week, tutoring a kindergarten student 2 hours a week and teaching a before school program 4 hours a week. The pay was ok but not quite enough to make ends meet. I still needed help from my mom, which I hated. That did not help with my depression, either. It made it worse. I felt like I was stuck in a rut with no way out. I was trying to make a living but not really living. I was just going through the motions day in and day out: wake up, work, eat, sleep, repeat.

When I moved away from Mankato, I thought I would have better opportunities in the teaching field, but I didn't. I couldn't handle having six or seven jobs at one time, anymore, so I left them all for a full-time job in a preschool. I loved the people I worked with but couldn't stand the preschool setting. I wanted to teach middle school kids who didn't need diaper changes and time outs. I searched for teaching jobs for ten years, but I had no luck.

When I was a massage therapist, I worked at Massage Envy to start; after I moved away from Aaron, I transferred to a closer location, but I didn't like it there so I quit. I found a salon to work at. The salon was full-service, so they did hair, nails, massages, facials and waxing. I actually worked at two locations when I started at the salon. I loved the environment and the services. I also loved trading massages to get my hair done. The problem was, I wasn't busy enough. I sat around not getting paid most days. We only got paid when we had clients, and during the week, I didn't have many. It was awful. Sitting around all day was extremely boring; I couldn't leave in case there was a walk in, and all I could do was laundry for the hair stylists or clean. I was bored and wanted something better. It's hard to make it as a massage therapist when you have no other source of income. When I went into massage therapy, I had the security of Aaron's income, but he broke it off before I was out of school, leaving me with a financial burden. Now that I was a single mom, again, I didn't have time to establish myself as a massage therapist. I needed to make money to support Isobelle.

Another problem with working at the salon was that I had to work mostly days because I needed to be home with my daughter, and those days weren't busy enough to make a living. My weekends were busy, but I could only work every other one. I needed to support Isobelle, but I wanted to be with her as well. It was a catch 22 situation. I had to make a decision. Keep on going as a massage therapist hoping to one day make really good money or find a steady paying job. I hated to leave massage therapy, but I chose the steady paying job so I could be there for my daughter. I took a job at a factory, which is where I still work. It's a good job, good benefits and money. It's not my dream, but it pays the bills.

For me, the bad part about having so many different jobs is that I felt like I was dying inside. Every time I left a job for whatever reason, I felt inadequate, like I wasn't doing life right. My mom stayed at jobs forever. She was at her last job before retirement for 17 years, and I know she hates when I want to start something new. It probably reminds her of my dad. She thinks I'm never satisfied with anything. She is somewhat right, so let's call a spade a spade. I'm not satisfied with merely any job. I want to live my passion, not settle for making ends meet.

My mom rarely agrees with my choices. I know she has always worried that I spend too much money and change my mind too much. I have learned to pick and choose what I tell her and what I keep to myself. I tend to tell my mom everything, so it's always been hard to keep things from her. She is always supportive and interested in what I am doing on the outside, but she silently judges. She doesn't mean to, but I can always see it on her face. When I take a new class or start something new, she always makes sure I'm not going to leave my factory job. I reassure her that I am not going to. It's a never-ending cycle. Because of this, I am afraid to tell anyone about any of my new endeavors. I feel like I am failing. I eventually give up. I wonder why I decided to take that class or start writing that book because it's not going to turn into anything. I fall into self-deprecating mode. Then I quit.

But now I tell myself every day who I am. I am an author. I am a healer. I am a teacher. Those are my "I am" speeches to myself. I added "I am an author" right before I started this book. I found an author program online and decided to go for it. The program seemed different than any other author class I had taken; I actually had to apply for it, not just sign up and pay, and I was ready to take the leap and apply. I wanted to see if I would be accepted. I was accepted, and they wanted my first book to be about my dealings with depression and addiction, and my first mission was to make a video of myself stating that I am an author. I can't tell you how liberating it was. Making that video was a scary first step; I don't even like to take selfies. I recorded it at least twenty times before I had the nerve to post it in my Facebook group. Yes, you heard that right, I posted it for my whole group to see, and this group has a lot of members. Once I took that leap, I felt amazing, like I was on top of the world, and I have written every day since posting the video. I've been writing for years but have never done anything with it, until now. I also have several books in waiting, and writing is the first thing I think about in the morning. When you tell yourself something that many times, eventually you begin to believe it. I am an author.

I regret having a lot of different jobs and relationships, but they all taught me something about myself. Each and every job and relationship I've had thus far has brought me closer to the person I am meant to be. Working with kids taught me patience. Working as a massage therapist taught me how to heal myself and others. Working in a factory taught me to be strong inside and out. Being in bad relationships taught me what I want and what I don't want in a relationship, and it taught me how to be happy even when I'm alone.

I am telling you this because some of you may have similar stories. Maybe you haven't found your dream job, either: the job you can't wait to do take on when you wake up in the morning. And if you don't currently have that job, going from job to job is not always a bad thing. You have to find what you like, and it may take a lot of different career paths to find the one that you love. That's ok. As long as you can make your life work while you are finding your dream job, then don't worry about it. I may not have a lot of money, but I make it work. I have always made sure my daughter has a roof over her head, food on the table and clothes on her back. If you struggle with finding your passion, know that we all do. Keep going. You will find it one day.

····· 9 ·····

Just Quit

The emptiness inside was like an explosion.

—Eleanor Clark

THEY SAY IT takes 21 days to create a habit. Do you ever wonder how long it takes to break that habit? A lifetime. It's also a lifelong struggle to create good habits.

After my breakup with Trevor, I was still living on my own in an apartment near my mom; I was not in a relationship and ready to focus on me. In theory. I still hated to be alone. I was buying liquor every week. I never went back on my antidepressants, though. I felt good for the most part. I would go to my mom's house to visit after work each day. We'd talk, have a couple drinks, and I'd go home to be with my daughter. I had liquor in my house, too. I'd have one or two more drinks before bed each night. I was still using alcohol to numb my pain and loneliness. I didn't want to stop or admit that I had a problem. I didn't think I did because I wasn't in a place where I wanted to injure myself anymore.

I spent my weekends at bonfires with my mom and her neighbors. I drank at those but not a lot. I only lived a few blocks away, so I figured it was fine for me to drive home. It probably wasn't, but I did it, anyway.

I also had bad hangovers, so bad that I couldn't get out of bed half the time. I'd spend the rest of the weekend laying around the house willing myself not to throw up and hoping the headaches would go away. I only got the hangovers when I was drinking with friends at my house. I drank more then because I knew I didn't have to drive.

I used to come home from work and need a drink. I mean really need one. I couldn't wait to get home and pour myself a drink. Today, I come home and either make a cup of tea or pour my soda over ice. I am happy with that, and I am saving a lot of money.

For me, it was the drinking alone that got me. I would say to myself, "I'm only having one drink today." One turned into two, which turned into three, and so on. A few days later, I'd find myself at the liquor store buying another bottle. I'd tell myself, "this is the last one," but it never was. My brain was telling me I needed a drink, so I listened.

Enough was enough. I made the choice to never drink alone, again. I told my brain to shut up when it told me to buy one more bottle. I had to tell it to shut up all the time. In fact, this past weekend I thought about buying a bottle of whiskey. What could one bottle hurt? he answer is *a lot*. I know myself; I wouldn't stop at one bottle. I'd be back at the store in a week for more. I chose to go home and pour myself a soda, instead. Best decision I made. I was in control. I didn't need a drink. I may have wanted one, but I didn't *need* it.

I have to take things one day at a time, shit, take things one *second* at a time when I have to. That phrase works for literally everything. There is no reason to look back on my past. That only makes me feel bad; looking too far into the future distracts me from the here and now. Right now is what I need to focus on. This second. Every second is special. I have decided to take a moment to enjoy it, to be in the now.

It is ok to mess up. It is ok to make mistakes. Mistakes happen so we can learn from them. You might make the same mistake over and over, but eventually you will learn to correct that mistake. The definition of insanity is doing the same thing over and over and expecting different results. Why did I think the result would change if I didn't change the action? I had to *want* to change. I had to be *willing* to change.

PART 4
LEARNING PROCESS

••••IO••••

Dis-Ease

Surround yourself with only people who are going to lift you higher.

—Oprah Winfrey

DEPRESSION AND ADDICTION are dis-eases. Dis-ease is a lack of ease or harmony in your body. Some people think dis-ease is a new age wacky concept, but I like it. I feel like it gives less power to the word "disease." Disease sounds so gross, like you have some sort of nasty ooze dripping out of your body. I would rather think that my body is not in harmony or alignment with my higher power.

To reiterate, depression and addiction are in fact a dis-ease. Many people do not agree with that statement. People who don't suffer from them often don't understand them. The main reason those of us who suffer from depression and/ or addiction don't seek help is because we are afraid that our friends and family won't understand. We are afraid of judgement and ridicule. We are afraid to admit that we are not at ease.

You may hear some people say, "Can't you just perk up and be happy?" If it were that easy, I wouldn't have a problem. It's not like flipping a switch on and off. When I am down, I am really down. It's not like I want to be depressed. I didn't ask for it. It merely happens.

This is the first time I have spoken about how bad my depression had gotten. I was afraid of being judged. I am still afraid of being judged. I have heard so many people say, "why would anyone kill themselves? It's so selfish." My mom is included in that, and I have heard her say that many times. I have to listen to it, knowing that I tried to kill myself more than once. Does that make me selfish? Maybe, but unless you have gone through tremendous pain, you have no idea what it does to your mind. It is natural for humans to want to escape pain in any way possible; it's human nature.

No person deals with grief in the same way. We all have our own ways of dealing with pain. If someone doesn't understand how depression feels, then they have no say in the matter. I am being harsh, but it's the truth. It is not their fault that they don't understand, and I am not trying to make anyone feel bad for it. I want them to understand that sometimes the pain can get so bad that we don't want to live anymore. I want them to understand how it can take over your mind and your body, how it can overwhelm you with pain, with physical and emotional exhaustion, with trying to hide your true feelings.

There were days when I wanted to stay in bed so I didn't have to deal with life. I wanted to be in the dark. I wanted to stay in my warm bed, away from the world. I still have days that I don't want to talk to anyone, but now it is because I choose to have some healthy alone time. I am not stuck to my bed, feeling pain and sorrow. I am not lonely; I am happy to be alone.

Emotional pain is worse than physical pain. With physical pain, you know why you are hurting. You know what happened to cause that pain. Emotional pain is harder to pinpoint. I had days that I cried for absolutely no reason. I had no idea what set it off or why I couldn't turn it off. I would wake up and lay there, not wanting to move, like I was paralyzed. I literally had to force myself to go to work, force myself to put a smile on my face, force myself to act like I was fine. Deep inside, I was falling apart. There was a black hole somewhere inside me, sucking out all of my joy.

You don't feel emotional pain in one regulated place, it's all over. Your whole body feels like a thousand pounds. I want to be perfectly clear. Those of us who suffer from depression and suicidal thoughts don't really want to die. We want the pain to stop. We want the suffering to stop. We want to feel normal. We don't want to walk through life like we are in purgatory.

Suicide attempts are not selfish but a cry for help. Yes, some people succeed at it. I am truly glad that I am not one of them. I believe that the ones who do succeed don't have anyone in their corner to turn to for help. They have no one to talk to. They are probably scared to talk to anyone. I know I was. The only person I told was my Doctor, and that is only because she saw the cuts. Had she not seen them; I wouldn't have told her. I was embarrassed, I thought there was something wrong with me and I couldn't control it. Why would I want to admit that I had something wrong with me? Why would anyone want to admit that? Especially when you are going to be judged for things that are out of your control.

Battling demons like depression and addiction take courage and sacrifice. You may have to cut people out of your life who don't support you. Cutting friends and family out of your life is very hard, but necessary. If they don't support you, they don't need to be in your life, for now. It doesn't have to be for-ever, although it could be. You have to focus on your healing. You don't have time for unsupportive people in your life. Take charge of who you let in.

Talking about your demons is hard work, and boy this is really hard for me right now. I haven't, until now, had the courage to come forward with my story. Knowing that my story will be out there for anyone to read is scary. Writing it brings up feelings that I have kept locked in the darkest parts of my mind, feelings I haven't felt in years. I am going through the pain all over again, bringing tears back into my eyes with each word I write. Knowing that you are reading the darkest parts of me is both terrifying and empowering.

I am finally getting it all out. I am stronger than I thought I was, and if I only help one person by writing my story, then it's all worth it. I am also helping myself by helping you.

•••• 11 ••••

Helping Distractions

Get busy living or get busy dying.

—The Shawshank Redemption

"GET BUSY LIVING or get busy dying" is one of my favorite quotes. It really comes down to that one sentence. You are either going to save yourself and start living or you are going to keep being miserable and die. Which is it going to be? Either way, you'll be busy doing one of them.

You may also have a similar decision to make. Maybe you dealt with a loss at a young age or felt the peer pressure harder than you wanted to. I encourage you to take an inventory of the moments in your life that could have led up to depression or addiction or even both. What happened to you? How did you deal with it? How are you dealing with it now? Life is perfectly messy and one hell of a ride. It's time to enjoy the ride, not fear it.

We all come to Earth to learn a lesson. In each lifetime our soul wants to learn something new. Your soul chooses where it wants to be and who it wants to become. After all, we are all souls borrowing a body. What we choose to do with that body can make us or break us.

How many of you put on a happy face so your friends and family will leave you alone? I did that for years until it got out of control. The more I drank, the more it numbed the sadness I felt. In reality, the alcohol was making the emptiness worse. Sitting alone in my house with a bottle of vodka was like being sucked into a black hole. My whole world was slipping into a dark pit of despair, and I was being eaten alive by the darkness. I didn't know it at the time, so I continued drinking. Today, I have learned how to control my addictions in many different ways. It is still a struggle, though. There are still days when I want to give up. I remind myself every day that I am worth it, my life has meaning, people need me and I am here for a reason.

I have found many ways to overcome my depression and addiction. There are so many things you can do to start living a life full of joy. The first step is to admit that you have a problem. I have a problem with alcohol. I have a problem with depression. Say it out loud. It's helpful to hear yourself say the words. Hearing your own voice say it gives the phrase power and meaning. It's one of the hardest things to do, but it is so powerful. The addiction has power over you, and by saying it out loud you are taking your power back.

Accept What Is, Strive for Better and Seek Support

God, grant me the serenity to accept the things I cannot change, courage to change the things I can and the wisdom to know the difference.

The serenity prayer is a helpful tool to help us slow down and embrace life. There are going to be things we can't change in our daily lives. We can't change how others act around us, but we can change the way we react to them. This prayer helps us think before we act. It helps me remember to breathe and to be in the moment. Stop and think before you say or do anything you will later regret.

When you can admit to yourself that you have an addiction and that you are depressed, you are ready to seek the help you need. When I admit to having depression and a problem with alcohol, I decided to take matters into my own hands first. I didn't seek the help of others even though I needed it because I was too proud.

After my parents moved to Arizona and I was living in their house, I found ways to distract myself from emotional pain. I learned how to crochet. I started with dish cloths and eventually moved into blankets. Focusing on making a blanket distracted me from feeling lonely and sad. The only problem was that it didn't distract me from having a drink. I would have one or two drinks while crocheting. It did, however, make me drink less. I was so determined to finish my project that I drank a lot slower. I saw that as a win. A small win, but a win all the same. Small victories are important during the recovery process. After a few months, I stopped making drinks while crocheting. Instead, I poured the soda and ice into my solo cup and had two or three of those. I only had alcohol on the weekends.

I've been to a few different AA meetings over the years. It's amazing how helpful it is to hear the stories of others. Knowing that other people struggle as much or more is comforting. It's a good feeling to realize that we are not alone. There is so much love and support in one room during these meetings that you never feel out of place or ashamed. You are never judged for the things you have done.

Idle Hands Are the Devil's Workshop

Find a few different hobbies that interest you. Have you heard the saying, "Idle hands are the devil's workshop"? It is when we settle down for the day that our addictions come out to play. For me, when I am relaxing at the end of the day, that is when my depression rears its ugly head. I'm sitting there, thinking, with nothing to do. I start getting sad, and then I want a drink or a smoke or something to eat. I know if I have a drink, I'll want a few more. If I have a snack, I'll have the whole bag of chips. If I have a smoke, I'll have one every hour. You get the point. Instead, get a hobby, keep your hands busy until it's time to sleep. I even play games on my phone to keep my hands busy. Keeping my brain and hands busy helped with cravings. I've noticed that when I am immersed in something, time seems to fly. Before I know it, it's time for bed.

My newest addiction is tea. I have three to five big cups of tea a day. Tea is so good for you; it's packed with antioxidants and flavor. I'm on my second cup of tea right now. It's superfood splash from David's Tea. I spend less money on tea than I did on alcohol, so that's a bonus. The tea lasts longer, too. Drinking a shit ton of tea during the day doesn't impair my judgment or make me do stupid things. Those of us with addictive personalities need to find healthy obsessions to fill our time.

Books, Movies and Television, Oh My

Reading is another way I helped myself. I read a lot of self-help books. I started with books about addiction and depression. I also read a lot of biographies, especially ones dealing with addiction. I found it helpful to read about other people's struggles. I could relate to them. It made me feel better to know that I wasn't the only one dealing with pain. I can see why we need to write about our pain, to connect with others, to free ourselves and to show other people that they are not alone. I wanted to know what other people went through and what they did to save themselves. I became mesmerized by the stories and the things the author did for one more drink or one more hit. Reading their stories made me feel like my life wasn't that bad. I had a roof over my head and food in the kitchen. Some people don't have those things. If those people could turn their lives around, so could I.

One of my favorite books about addiction is *The Heroin Diaries* by Nikki Sixx. For those of you who don't know who Nikki Sixx is, he's in the band Motley Crue. The book is literally his journal that he wrote while high on heroin. He gets down and dirty with you and makes you feel like you are right there with him. I love it because it's real and it's raw, you can feel the pain he was in. Nikki is brutally honest about his past, his dark side and his suffering. He shares his deepest, darkest secrets. His life was messy, but he managed to change it, and he made me feel as if I could, too.

I also got into fantasy-fiction. I read *Harry Potter, Twilight, House of Night* and *A Shade of Vampire*. I love getting immersed in a fantasy world; it's a break from reality. Magic and vampires are my favorite. I like the end-of-the-world books like *The Hunger Games, Divergent* and *Maze Runner*. Those are only a few of the series that I have read. There are too many to name. I would get so wrapped up in the story that I would forget about my own life. I wouldn't want to stop reading. When I would finish a series, I felt sad, like I was missing a part of my life. I had to find another series to fill the void. When I read, I can't do anything else until I finish the book. I like series books so I can't stop until I read the whole series. I had to take a break so I could focus on writing.

Finding little ways to distract yourself from reality for a while is good, especially when you are home alone and all you can think about is how sad you are or how much you want a drink or drug. In the beginning, it's essential to stay distracted from your desire to drink, do drugs or harm yourself. Soon you realize that the hours are passing and you haven't felt the urge to do anything harmful. Some days will be harder than others, believe me. I still have days where I want to crawl into a hole and die, but I remind myself that I can get past the feelings. I can overcome the pain and the fear.

One other method of distraction I use is television or movies. It's like a book. You get hooked on the show and have to know what's going to happen next. I like to mix up my shows. Some days I need something funny, and other days I like drama. I have learned to limit my TV time, though. For a while, I was watching episode after episode of whatever show I was into and didn't get anything else done. I also have a problem with eating while watching TV I'll have a small snack, which turns into a bag of chips and a couple of cookies. I was gaining weight like no tomorrow. Something had to change. I started playing Match Three games while the TV was on. It works really well. My hands are too busy for food.

If you think about it, what you are really doing is replacing one addiction for another. Those of us who suffer from addictive personalities need the addiction to get through life. The bottom line is that you have to find a healthy addiction. Smoking and drinking go hand in hand. It was once thought that quitting one bad habit at a time is better than trying to quit all of them. This is not the case, anymore. We are more likely to want a drink when we are smoking and vice versa. Research now states that it is better for the recovery process to quit all of the unhealthy addictions at the same time. Most recovery centers encourage it now and are equipped to help us abstain from multiple addictions at once. Plus, your body will thank you for it.

Get a Dog (Or a Cat or a Horse)

I grew up with a cat, and I had a cat and dog when I was married. I am definitely a cat person, but I loved my dog. She was the best dog in the world, so friendly and easy to take care of. Since I wasn't able to have pets, my ex kept both when we split. I was heartbroken. I wasn't allowed to have a cat or dog in the low-income place, but when I moved back to my hometown area in 2009, I was able to have a pet. I was so excited to have a pet again. My daughter and I decided to get a cat as our pet. We picked her out when she was just a few weeks old. Actually, I think she picked us. I decided on a cat because I didn't have time for a dog, and it wouldn't have been fair to the dog.

Pets help so much with depression. Lily, my cat, knows when I am sad. She senses when I need her to cuddle with me. Lily is a blessing. I talk to her like she is human, and she talks back. I have no idea what she is saying, and she probably has no idea what I am saying, so it works out. She has to be the most resilient cat. I have moved her from place to place so many times, but she takes it in stride and is always happy. Lily is my rock. She follows me around like a dog and only leaves me alone when she needs a nap. When I am writing, she is usually climbing over my lap back and forth, making it hard to type, butting her head into mine and licking my face and arms. Sometimes I have to tell her to knock it off so I can get some work done. I have not been lonely since she came into my life. My daughter once asked me if I ever get lonely when she's gone. I told her, "sometimes." She looked at Lily in my lap and laughed. She said, "No, you have Lily, you treat her like she's your best friend."

She's right, Lily is my best friend of the four-legged variety. She keeps me sane and makes me happy. Did you know that you can get a cat as an emotional support animal? The fair housing act allows you to live with your ESA even in "no-pets" apartments. You can even bring your ESA on an airline when you travel. All you need is the correct paperwork. An ESA is not like a service animal because they don't have training to provide emotional support; it's in their nature.

Parenting a pet is great for our mental health. Emotional support animals can help with depression, anxiety, post -traumatic stress disorder, stress and can also help with sleep. ESA's also provide a cure for loneliness. I'm not sure there are rules stating that it has to be a cat or a dog, either. I bet you could consider any animal an ESA as long as he or she is providing you with emotional support.

There are things to consider before picking out a cat as an ESA. I focus on cats because I know the most about them. I recommend having an indoor cat as an ESA. I had an outdoor cat when I was married. I didn't want him to be an outdoor cat, but he couldn't help it. He was drawn to the outdoors. Outdoor cats are more wild than indoor cats. My cat was outside more than inside. He would leave in the morning and not come home until nighttime. He was always defensive, like he always had to watch his back. He got into a lot of fights with other animals, so he hissed a lot. He was friendly to me for the most part. He liked to sleep on my pillow, but if I moved too much, he would bite me. Not to say he wasn't a good cat, he mostly was, but he did not provide emotional support.

Lily has been an indoor cat her whole life. She has no interest in the outdoors, and she only bites when she is playing. She feels bad when she play-bites, so she stops, licks the spot and purrs. She is definitely an ESA for me.

Breed and age are other factors to consider. Some breeds of cats are naturally wild and independent, while other breeds like a lot of attention. My cat is a tabby/calico short hair. Mixed breed cats make good ESA's because they are less temperamental. You can find a list of the best ESA cats online.

You'll want to consider the age of your ESA as well. Sometimes older cats are temperamental and have a harder time adjusting to your home. You may have to spend a fair amount of time getting to know your adult cat and letting it get to know you. If you have the time to spend with him or her, that is great, adult cats need good homes.

I highly recommend adopting an emotional support animal for depression. I don't know where I would be without my Lily. I love getting home from work and seeing how excited Lily is to see me. An ESA gives you the unconditional love you deserve.

Meditate

I learned a lot from my massage classes. Most classes would start with a meditation. I learned how to meditate before school but didn't do it often. Starting each class with a meditation got me back into the practice. Meditation is good for your soul. It helps your mind to settle down and brings you into deep relaxation. It takes some practice to calm your body and mind down, but once you get the hang of it, it's easy.

I started with just a few minutes each day, usually with a guided meditation. I found that it was easier to relax with someone guiding me through it. If you are anything like me, you can't sit still for very long. I am always moving. I get an itch somewhere, get uncomfortable or lose focus. If that sounds like you, don't worry, meditating gets better. Start with one minute. Sixty seconds is easy to accomplish. It may not sound like much, but it works. All you need to do is find a comfortable place to sit or lie down, close your eyes and take long deep breaths. You probably won't be able to clear your mind at first, but eventually you will get there. I like to use the app called Insight Timer on my phone. The app has thousands of free meditations ranging from one minute to an hour or more. The one-minute guided meditations focus on breathing. When I first started, I did my one-minute meditation as soon as I woke up. It's a good start to the day. Once you get the hang of it, work up to five minutes then ten minutes and longer if you feel the urge.

It was hard for me at first. I had a love-hate relationship with meditating. I loved the way it made me feel, like I was ready to face the day with a clear head and an open mind. But I hated having to sit still. I made a vow to meditate every day for twenty-one days. I wanted to make meditating a habit. I added one minute to my morning routine every day until my morning meditation was ten minutes. I couldn't do more than ten minutes in the morning because I didn't want to wake up any earlier. After a week, I added a meditation to my night time ritual. I successfully created my new habit.

In the beginning, I always chose guided meditations. There was something about being guided into a paradise that made meditating easier for me. I don't use guided meditation much anymore. I find that plain music from the insight timer works best for me now. When I meditate before bed, I choose music with binaural beats to help with my dreams. I fall asleep to it and have the most vivid dreams. I've always had vivid dreams, but with the music, I remember them better and they are more vivid. My morning routine varies. I sometimes do a five-minute guided meditation and sometimes I sit on the edge of my bed with my eyes closed and breathe for a minute or two. That was how I started to create my habit. Now that I have my habit established, I merely find a meditation that suits me for that day and go with it.

Insight Timer has guided meditations ranging from weight loss to anxiety and depression to making money to finding your passion and much more. You can find a meditation for pretty much anything your heart desires. YouTube is another great source for free meditations and another great free site I like to use is Fragrant Heart. I love that there are so many free meditation resources out there. Insight Timer is by far my favorite. There is an option to pay for the service also. The paid version lets you rewind, fast forward and pick up where you left off. The paid version also has courses you can take whenever you want. You can pay for individual courses in the free version as well. I haven't paid for a subscription yet but have been considering it. When you sign up for the paid version, the money helps keep the app free for those who can't afford it.

Meditation is proven to help fight depression, addiction, anxiety, PTSD, bipolar disorder and many other illnesses. The power of the mind is a beautiful thing. Keep your mind strong and healthy with a daily dose of meditation.

Jamming Out

Listening to music is another way to keep your mind busy. Music can be a tricky business. When I was in my deep depression, I would listen to sad music, and it made the depression worse. I wanted to remain sad; I thought it was what I deserved. Choosing the right music when you are trying to pull yourself out of a funk is critical. Any song that triggers a sad memory will sink you. Today's technology is great for music therapy. You are able to build your own playlist so you don't have to add songs that trigger your depression. Back in the 90s, we had cassette tapes and CDs. There was only skip or fast forward. Hearing the beginning riff was inevitable. If you're anything like me, the beginning riff of certain songs trigger sad memories, and I find myself feeling down. Now that you can make your own playlist, it's easy to choose only music that doesn't trigger a negative emotional response. Find songs that speak to you, songs you can relate to. I love the song by Pink, "F**kn' Perfect". I used to listen to it over and over when I was deep in depression. The whole song is about not feeling good enough and going through bad times. The chorus says, "don't ever feel less than fuckin' perfect, you are fuckin' perfect to me."Listening to that song makes me feel better, It makes me feel like someone knows I am perfect exactly the way I am.

For several years, I was unable to listen to certain songs because they reminded me of men who hurt me, me hurting myself or my angels in heaven. I couldn't listen to *Don't Speak* by No Doubt for many years. It was the song Alex (my first love) and I had together. Every time I heard that song it brought me back to all the pain I felt during that time of my life. I couldn't listen without crying. During my deep depression, the crying turned into me hurting myself. I have a ton of memories like that with songs. Depression triggers a strong urge to stay down. Instead of building yourself back up, you do things that keep you down. For me, it was listening to sad songs, crying and writing poetry.

It's hard to pull yourself out of a funk, but it can be done. Try not to listen to music that triggers a negative response. Choose happy and upbeat songs that make you smile and want to dance. Start by finding one song that inspires you to get up and dance, to sing at the top of your lungs. Listen to it over and over. Get up and dance to the beat, and sing loud. It might sound silly, but it's effective. I like to sing at the top of my lungs all the time. I don't care who hears me. I do it at work all the time.

Connect Through Music, Technology, and Social Groups

Don't Speak, still brings me to a time when I was heartbroken, but it also helps me remember that I went through the pain and came out the other side stronger. Now, I love the song, once again.

If you aren't a music person or need a break from it, try a podcast. There are millions of inspiring podcasts to dive into. The topics are vast and range from spirituality to horror and everything in between. I like to mix it up from day to day. I love the horror/scary podcasts. They keep me on my toes and make me think. My favorite horror podcast is called *Pleasing Terrors* with Mike Brown. I also like to learn about metaphysical stuff, so I listen to a podcast called *Psychic Teachers* with Deb Bowen and Samantha Fey. Some days I opt for funny. On those days, I just search for funny podcasts and pick one. It's hard to recommend humor podcasts since everyone has a different sense of humor. I will tell you that there is a podcast for everyone, though, you just have to find what you like.

I recently found a podcast called The Hilarious World of Depression. It's full of interviews with many comedians who suffer from depression. Hearing their stories is awesome. I can always relate to them. They give great advice, and it's full of humor. Depression is not funny, but it *is* funny. The comedians make light of the not so light subject. One of the episodes I listened to today was about giving your depression a name. You give it a name and then describe it as if your depression was a person. When you start to feel negative thoughts forming, tell Joe or Kelly to "Shut Up!" The episode was more in-depth than that, but it's the basic gist. Giving your depression a name makes it a separate entity. It's not who you are, it's your depression monster.

Getting out there and meeting new people is a great way to find like-minded friends and people who may have gone through something like you have. There is an awesome app called Meetup. It is filled with groups who meet for conversations and classes on topics that you are interested in. You put in your location, and it finds the groups for you.

It's important in the recovery process to find people who can relate to you and help you. I belong to several Facebook groups who share stories like mine and have similar interests. Most of the people I have yet to meet in person, but that's ok.

The things they share are helping me nonetheless. I can't tell you how much it helps to meet people with a story similar to mine. Reading about it is one thing, but talking about it is even better. Whether it's in person or over the phone via text, Skype, email or phone call, talking to someone eases the guilt and loneliness you feel for the things you've done. Everyone has a journey, and sharing yours could be life-saving. You have no idea how your words will affect someone. Maybe all that person needs is to know that you have gone through what they are going through and that you made it. You could save a life, and you could be saved yourself. Get out there and meet new people. Surround yourself with positive friends and let the negative ones go.

Quiet Your Mind, Change Your Thoughts

Those of us with addictions and depression are drawn to chaos; it follows us around. Learning to avoid people and chaotic situations is important to our well-being. During my worst days, I surrounded myself with so much chaos that it was eating me alive. I had to be around people who were bad for me in order to have fun. I would always regret it eventually. It is hard to leave that chaos behind. The chaos distracts our minds; it helps to shut out the pain we feel on a daily basis. We have to learn to sit quietly with our thoughts and accept them.

It is all about mindset during recovery. Without the proper mindset, we will keep going in circles and never learn to be alone. We call ourselves fat, stupid, ugly and pathetic on a daily basis. I have always had a problem with self-esteem. I looked in the mirror every day and told myself I was ugly, fat and don't deserve love. I tore myself down so much that I learned to believe that I really was undeserving of love from anyone. The more negative self-talk we do, the more our minds learn to believe it. We can't love anyone else until we learn to love ourselves. We can't love ourselves until we learn to accept who we are as individuals. When you tell yourself a hundred or more times a day that you aren't good enough, you won't be good enough.

Turn the negative self-talk into positive self-talk. It's not easy. In fact, it's actually really uncomfortable. As human beings, we learn at a young age to be negative about ourselves and others. We put others down to make ourselves feel better. When someone puts you down, it's because that is what they don't like about themselves.

For those of you with kids. You know how when your child puts themselves down, it makes you cringe inside, right? When my daughter says she is fat, I jump right in to tell her that she is not. I wonder why she thinks that; she's not even close to being fat. Then I remember, she gets it from me. I taught her to think that she is fat with my own insecurities. I am always saying how fat I look or how an outfit makes me look like a cow. It's no wonder she thinks she's fat, too. It's a horrible feeling to know that I did that to my kid. So, it is really important to change our own thinking in order to help our kids and the other people around us to feel good about themselves, too.

You may think that it's too late to change your mindset, but it's not. It is never too late. You really can teach an old dog new tricks, but that old dog has to be willing to change. Change won't happen overnight; it is a gradual thing that happens over time. Take weight, for example. If you are overweight, you didn't become overweight in a couple of days; you slowly gained more weight over time. It took me ten years to gain the weight back that I had lost during my divorce. I hated myself. I hated how I looked. No diet worked for me. I also had the mindset that I was fat and the mindset that I wanted to lose weight fast. It took me ten years to put all that weight back on, so why did I think it would only take a couple of weeks to lose it?

I had to change my mindset first. Nothing was going to work until I accepted myself. In 2016, I learned new ways to change my mindset. I studied affirmations and emotional freedom technique (EFT). Daily affirmations work really well to help you to start changing your mindset. When I started, I would write down positive things on a sticky note and put them on my bathroom mirror so that each time I was in the bathroom, I could read them. Looking at yourself in the mirror when you say nice things about yourself is even more affirming. Yes, it's awkward at first. I felt stupid doing it, but I made myself. I was determined to learn how to love myself.

My affirmations started with small, easy to remember phrases. I am good enough. I am smart enough. I am beautiful. I am kind. I am unique. I said them all the time. I would even repeat them to myself at work when I remembered. They didn't work right away; it took a long time for me to accept myself. I was still using negative statements as well. The trick is to listen to your thoughts. When you hear yourself saying something negative, change it to a positive statement. Our minds are constantly thinking whether you realize it or not. It's hard to keep track of your thoughts throughout the day. The more you do it, the easier it becomes. One day it will come naturally to you. It will be something you do without thinking about it.

Daily affirmations are legit. It takes time to retrain your brain to believe them, but it does work. It's weird at first. Your brain will fight you, tell you it's not right. That's ok. Think about how many times you tell yourself that you aren't good enough, not pretty enough, skinny enough or smart enough. You believe it right? It's time to turn the negative statements into positive ones. It's the same concept. We are so wired to talk negatively to ourselves that when we finally say something positive it feels unnatural.

EFT (emotional freedom technique) is an effective technique, too. Another name for it is tapping. You tap pressure points in the face, collar bone, arm and hand while saying different affirmations. There are many YouTube videos that have you follow along with a teacher. You can use EFT for pain, addictions, depression, anxiety, manifestation and much more. I went to a therapy session a few times for one on one EFT training for my depression. It was amazing. I tapped my way through a lot of pain during those sessions. I won't lie, it was emotionally exhausting. I cried a lot during the sessions, and things I didn't know I felt came to the surface, but I left feeling uplifted. A weight had been lifted from my soul. I like the YouTube videos, but a one on one session was much more powerful. Having someone walk me through the process step by step and holding my hand while I sobbed was comforting. If you are going to try EFT, check out the videos first, but definitely find a local EFT certified therapist. You won't regret it.

Relaxing Massage

As a massage therapist, I have learned that massage is not only effective in relieving physical pain but also emotional pain. Massage creates endorphins and oxytocin. It only takes fifteen minutes of massage for the endorphins to kick in. Endorphins reduce pain and create a euphoric state. Getting a massage at least once a month by a professional is recommended. I can tell you from experience it really does help. I only had one massage before I went to school for it; now I try to get one as much as I can. I don't practice anymore as you know, but I know how beneficial they are. If you feel you can't afford one, it's ok. I don't get them as often as I'd like for that reason, so I just get them as much as I can, and there are plenty of at home techniques you can do. Reflexology on your feet is as beneficial as a full body massage. Your feet have pressure points that connect to all the organs and muscles of the body. All you need is a tennis ball. Put the tennis ball under your foot and roll it back and forth. You can use as much pressure as you can handle. Doing that each day for fifteen minutes will release those endorphins and make you feel better. You can even place the tennis ball under a knot in your shoulder and lay on it or lean into a wall. Stretching is also a form of massage. I like to stretch before and after work every day. It keeps the blood flowing and helps to decrease injury. You can find a lot of massage tools on Amazon that are really great for self-care. Try a few things and see what works best for you.

Crystals 101

I love crystals; I carry them in my pocket every day. I have some in my purse and all over my house; I even have them in my car. Crystals are magical and healing. I choose different crystals to carry each day depending on my mood. Blue crystals are good for communication. They are linked to the throat chakra. I like to carry amazonite for communication while at work. There are many great crystals for depression. Sunstone is a wonderful mood lifter. It helps bring positive energy into your life. Citrine absorbs negative energy. Smoky quartz absorbs your negative thought patterns. Rose quartz brings soothing and healing energy to your heart chakra. Carnelian reduces anxiety and gives you a good energy boost. Amethyst is one of my favorite crystals. It transmutes negative energy into positive energy and heals emotional pain. Those are the easiest crystals to find and fairly inexpensive. You can find tons of information about crystals online. Taking care of your crystals is important. Cleanse them in sage smoke, the moonlight or sunlight at least once a month. Cleansing helps keep the crystals charged. If you would like to try crystals, I suggest starting with rose quartz and amethyst. They have gentle energy and are very effective. A good book to use when discovering crystals is *The Crystal Bible* by Judy Hall, and there are three or four editions.

Essential Oil Baths

Finally, after a long day, take a nice hot bath with Epsom salt and essential oils. I recommend lavender to start with if you are unfamiliar with oils. Some oils can be harmful if used improperly. Lavender is good for soothing sore muscles and relaxation. Baths are relaxing and calming after a hard day. When you drain the tub, you can visualize all of your worries and pain going down the drain. Wash the day away.

One of the biggest things you can do in your recovery is celebrating your wins no matter how small. Treat yourself to a nice meal or some new clothes; go to a movie or do something that you normally wouldn't do. Enjoy those wins!

••••12••••

Finding Passion

There is nothing permanent except change.

—Heraclitus

AS HUMANS, WE are always learning and evolving. Change happens to us every day, and we can either choose to roll with the punches or freak out. If you are anything like me, you love change. I've lived in a lot of different houses in my life. Each time I have moved I have gotten rid of a little bit more stuff. My favorite thing to do is purge. I hate clutter, so I am always finding things to donate. I do the same thing with jobs. When a job starts to become boring, I move on.

I know why I liked changing places and jobs; it's because I hadn't found my passion yet. I hadn't found the place where I feel at home, and I hadn't found the career I love. I don't feel like I belong in Minnesota, this place does not speak to my heart. My heart yearns for warmth, water and sun. My soul wants to be outdoors all year round.

I will be forty years old soon, and I have finally found the passion that makes me want to jump out of bed just itching to work. I was constantly taking classes and getting different certifications, hoping that the next class I took would be the one that sparks my passion. I know so many people who love waking up to do their job. I wake up and go to work to put food on my table. It's just a means to an end for me, nothing more. My writing and publishing program is the work that sparked my passion. I can finally say that I am excited to work; work on my books, work on coaching programs and work on helping you.

Finding your passion can be a long, hard process. It's even harder for those of us with depression and addiction issues. I get excited about a new class I am taking, hoping that I will love it and be able to make a living doing it. I finish the course that promises I will start making money right away, only to find out I don't know how to market myself. You see, all the courses I take are work -for-yourself jobs; what they don't tell you is that the clients don't fall out of the sky and into your lap. Most of the courses don't have a step by step program teaching you how to find and keep clients while you are feeding your entrepreneurial spirit.

Take me, for example. I have been writing on and off since I was a little kid. I self-published one book on Amazon in 2011 thinking I would make it big. I sold maybe five books. I had no idea how to market it, and I didn't get it professionally edited. I knew nothing about publishing. So, I gave up for a while. A few years later, I got another idea for a book. I started writing it until I got stuck and gave up on the project before I even finished it. A few years later, I did the same thing. Had an idea, started writing and gave up. Throughout the whole process, I knew in the back of my mind I didn't know anything about publishing a book. It wasn't the writing that made me give up, it was that I knew I wouldn't do anything about it so I asked myself: *why finish?*

I did the same thing with classes. I would come across a class that sounded interesting to me, plus it was guaranteed to make me money. I would then contemplate if I should spend the money, ultimately deciding that I should. I would sign up, get excited to start and be really into it. I would always complete the classes but have never done anything with them. I put the work into learning, but I don't put the work into actually making a living from it. My mind is always excited to learn but afraid to put myself out there.

It's the same with addiction. You can't expect to change if you don't put in the work. You have to be ready for the change and be willing to admit you need help. Until you decide that you are ready for a change, you are going to keep running on a hamster wheel hoping the change will happen to you. That's not how it works. If you want to see results, put in the work.

Teaching was never a passion of mine. I got a degree in it because my mom and brother wanted me to go to college. I loved taking classes and working toward my degree; in fact, I think I liked working toward the *imagined* outcome better than the *actual* outcome. If you remember from a previous chapter, I couldn't find a full-time job as a teacher. My spirits were low, and I gave up. I believe that if teaching was really for me, I wouldn't have given up. I would have tried harder to find a teaching job. At the time, I thought I was trying hard, but something inside me was holding me back. I didn't really want to be a teacher. I honestly didn't know what I wanted. It's an uncomfortable feeling: not knowing who you are or what you want to do with your life.

I knew in the back of my mind that I was meant for greater things. I was meant to help not only kids but adults as well. I wasn't meant to be stuck in a nine to five job. I have always had an urge to write, but something always got in the way. And people got in the way. I was told many times, "you can't make a living as a writer," and I was always discouraged from writing. I didn't stop, though. I wrote poems and short stories every now and then. I wrote in a journal and a dream diary. I took a children's writing course in 2005 and self-published an adolescent novel based on addictions. As I said, it didn't do well, but I was writing.

From 2004 to 2013 nothing seemed to be going my way. I couldn't sell my book, and teaching wasn't for me. I was given a nice camera, so I thought I'd take a course to learn photography. I loved it. I worked as a photographer at one of those family places, and I even won an award for my creativity. I didn't want to work for someone, though, and I wanted to have my own business. I did a few weddings and kids photo shoots on the side, and I was happy, or so I thought. I couldn't seem to obtain enough clients to quit my studio job and, unfortunately, I lost my camera in my breakup with Kevin. He took the camera since he bought it. It was a birthday present, but I guess he wanted to hurt me by taking it back. That ended my career in photography. I didn't have the means to buy a new camera, so I quit, instead. I probably could have saved up for one, but I didn't. Photography wasn't my passion, either.

I was beginning to lose faith that I even had a passion. I felt like I wasn't good at anything. I didn't have a special talent. I only dabbled in a million different things, so I went back to teaching for a while. I wanted to use the degree my grandparents paid for, but I still wasn't happy with what I was doing.

When I chose to go to school for massage therapy, I thought that would be my passion. I loved helping people with their pain. I was a healer in more than one way. I healed their sore muscles, but I also healed their spirits. I wasn't only a massage therapist; I was a personal therapist. My clients asked for advice, confided in me and respected me. I was good at massage, but it still didn't feel right. I thought I wanted my own practice. In a way I did, but not specifically massage. I was still trying to figure out what made me really passionate.

I learned about essential oils. I became a member of a direct selling company in hopes I could start a business. I wasn't good at that, either. I am not much of a salesperson. I was pretty good at talking about which oils to use for home remedies. I never got the knack for asking people to buy them, though. I also learned how to read angel cards, tarot cards and akashic records. I had a lot of practice clients for that but didn't know what to do with it after I was certified.

I have always been afraid to leave a nine to five job for fear of the unknown. I needed a steady paycheck in order to support my daughter. I wanted to do all these things as a side hustle until I could make it a regular job, but by the time I was home from my day job, I was too tired to bother with it. I have always thought it would be awesome to have a job where I could get paid to take and rate courses; that way I'd always be learning and getting paid to do it. But I think that it was distracting me from a more focused vision; these habits led me to knowing a lot about a lot of things but being the master of none. I needed to stop dabbling and start focusing on one thing, the one passion that makes me the happiest.

Throughout all of the courses I was taking and the trades I was learning, my mind always came back to writing. I wanted to be an author so badly. Writing is the one thing I never stopped thinking about. I have so many unfinished books, so many ideas for more, my brain won't stop telling me to write. Better yet, my soul won't let it go. It's about time I started to listen to them.

I had been looking for my passion in all the wrong places. I should have been looking inside myself to find it. It was right there, staring me in the face. The one thing I never gave up on. Writing. I took a lot of breaks from writing, but I never stopped imagining my life as an author. It only took me twenty years to figure out that writing is my real passion.

I literally laughed out loud just now in amazement as I write that. It may have taken twenty years to figure it out, but who cares?! It doesn't matter how long it takes to find your passion. It might take you a year, ten years, fifty years, the point is to never stop searching until you find what drives you.

I used to try manifesting my dreams. Manifesting is when you truly believe that you already have what you want. You envision yourself with it, paint a picture of what your life looks like with whatever it is you want, whether it be a job, a product or a lifestyle. I would make vision boards and recite affirmations. Manifesting can be really easy, and everyone can do it. The problem I had with manifesting my passion was I wasn't putting in the work. I thought I could manifest it into existence without lifting a finger. Everyone else was doing it, so why couldn't I? I did manifest a few small things. I wanted a new car so I could give mine to my daughter. My parents bought a new car and sold me their old one. It happened a month after I started trying to manifest it. I figured I could manifest my dream job, too. My dream job for the past twenty years has been author. I thought if I put it out there to the universe, I would get inspired to write. I did my vision board and affirmations about four years ago. I have written in that four years but didn't know where to go with it. It wasn't working. I'd write, give up, write, give up and so on for years. I was not going to become an author without doing the work. This book wasn't writing itself!

Then one day, it happened. I found the course that changed my life, is *still* changing my life, the course that is helping me write this book: an all in one course for writing, publishing and marketing my book. There is finally an end game in sight. It gives me motivation to write, guidance, support and a great community of like-minded people. I took one last chance on my dream, and when I signed up for it, I said, "this is it; if it doesn't work, I'm done." Well, guess what? It's working. Since I signed up, I haven't stopped writing.

Finally, a step by step course that has helped me make my dream come true. I guess the manifestation did work. It took longer than I expected, but it worked!

Never give up on your dreams. They are your dreams for a reason. When the same idea keeps popping into your head, it is because you are meant to do something with it. You will never be happy if you give up. When you start to doubt yourself, take a step back and reassess the situation. Ask yourself: "what is my long- term goal?" and aim for that.

Deadlines and Distractions

I have had tons of setbacks from fulfilling my dream of being an author. I had them while writing this book. My goal was to write a certain amount of words each day, and some days were better than others. Some days I didn't write in this book at all, and some days I had to make myself stop so I could get some sleep before my day job. I still tried to write something each day, even if it wasn't on this book. I didn't throw in the towel but picked it back up the next day and wrote as much as I could. It didn't matter if I didn't meet my specific goal for each day. I kept working on it and set deadlines for myself.

Setting a deadline kept me on track. A deadline kept me focused, it was something to work toward. If I didn't have a deadline, then there was nothing telling me to keep going. The book I started before this one is not done. I didn't have a deadline or a daily goal. I was writing whenever I felt the urge, and most days, I didn't have the urge to write. There was no end game for that book. Once I learned that I had to set goals and deadlines for writing, it became a job for me. A job I love to do a job I can't wait to do.

What about distractions? I am the queen of distractions and procrastination. Today's world is so crazed with distractions, it's hard to get anything done. We have phones, computers, tablets, a million TV channels, and let's not forget the housework that can't wait. On top of those distractions, some of us have kids who are forever bored or need to be somewhere. Some days I would want to come home from work and veg out in front of the TV or play a game on my phone, and some days I would do just that. I would decide to play a game for twenty minutes, twenty minutes turned into two hours, and then it was time for dinner. Even now, I have noticed that when I turn on the TV or play a game, I get addicted to it. I don't want to stop. Then I tell myself, "I'll do better tomorrow." Distracting myself has never gotten me what I wanted, in fact, it has stopped me from doing the things that I am actually passionate about. So, I decided to create better habits. I used to look at my computer and groan. Now, instead of groaning, I decide to get my work done for the day *then* relax with a TV show or game. There is no reason I need to watch more than one or two episodes a day or play a game for more than thirty minutes. It feels so good to be in command of my time and to feel that sense of accomplishment when I *use* my time instead of wasting it.

So, again, accomplish your daily goal first, reward yourself later. If you do it today, you will feel accomplished. You won't beat yourself up. If you keep telling yourself you'll do better tomorrow, tomorrow may never come. On the flip side, don't beat yourself up if you are having an off day. It's ok to take a break, we all need breaks. Give yourself a day to relax and give 110% tomorrow. But make sure your tomorrow comes. Pick up that task, and get it done.

Secondly, schedule your time and get organized. Scheduling a time to work on your passion will help you to resist distractions. I like to plan my writing times in segments. I block out an hour to start. I keep the TV off. I use the "do not disturb" feature on my phone and allow phone calls from my daughter and mom only instead of turning it off entirely purely in case of an emergency. But if you can turn it off entirely, better yet! I also suggest finding a personal place to work. If you have an office or spare room, turn it into your workspace. If you don't have extra space in your house, get creative. A small corner of your house works perfectly. Find a desk or make your own. I turned my kitchen table into a desk when I didn't have space. My daughter and I eat at the counter or on the couch, so the table worked for me. Put a few decorations on the desk. I like crystals that help with writing, a vase with flowers and a few inspiring books. Try to keep the clutter out of your space and keep it organized. I don't know about you, but when I see clutter, I have to organize it before I can get anything done. By the time I'm done organizing, I'm not in the mood to work anymore.

Let your family know when you block out time to work on the things you are passionate about. Since you want to be free from distractions, your family is included in the distraction column. I can't tell you how many times my daughter wants to talk to me when I'm in the zone. I let her know that I am going to be busy for at least an hour, maybe more. Treat it like your regular job. People don't bother you at a nine to five job unless it's an emergency, so they need to follow the same respect for your new job. Your passion is actually *more* than just a job, so treat it that way. Pretty soon your passion will be a full-time gig, so start letting your loved ones know that you need time to put in the work.

Making Time

It can be really hard to find time to work on a passion that is either bringing in a small amount of money or none at all. Most of us are already working forty hours a week, so taking even more time away from family can be challenging. If you really want to make your passion your career, then you will have to put in the time. It won't be forever; eventually things will calm down, and hopefully you can leave your nine to five job. For now, put in the hours. You'll thank yourself for it later. Think about this, if you devote one hour a day to your passion, that is only seven hours a week. Can you spare seven hours a week for your passion? Can you use seven hours a week for something you know will make you happy? There are twenty-four usable hours in every day, so use them wisely. Yes, you need sleep. Most adults really only need seven to eight hours of sleep a night. You work eight hours a day, sleep eight hours, there are still eight hours left. What are you doing with those eight hours? Are you responsible for all of the chores around the house? Are you wasting time watching television? Do you procrastinate? Or are you just too exhausted? Even if you have taken that responsibility on, it's time to delegate. Have your family help out. There is no reason your kids or partner can't help out around the house. Start using your time wisely. This is your dream, make it happen!

Follow Your Dream

Never let anyone crush your dream. There are going to be people who try to tell you that you won't make it, your dream is unreasonable, you'll never make money with that, you should keep your day job, and many more painful things. I've heard them all. I've even heard, "why would you want to leave that job, you have it made there!" Maybe I do have it made, maybe my day job is easy peasy, and I make good money. The question becomes, am I happy? If the answer is "no," then it isn't my dream job.; it's a job that keeps a roof over my head and food on my table. That's all. Do you have a similar experience?

Who are the people in your life telling you that you won't make it? Those are the people you can't tell about it. Maybe not forever, but for now. When someone makes you feel bad for wanting to better yourself, then they don't deserve to be included in that part of your life. It's ok to keep that part of your life a secret from the people who don't support you. There will be a time to let them in on your secret life if you chose to do so. Your confidence will kick in, you will feel at peace with your decision and you will be living your dream life. It's not an "I told you so" moment, it's an "I did it" moment that you will feel so strongly within that you won't even feel the need to tell them at all, they will just see it.

When people see others succeed when they are not, they can become crabs in the bucket trying to pull the escapees back in. They may become jealous that you did it. Conversely, you might find that your friends and family now want your help in living their dream life. Even in this elevated state, it is still easy to become cocky at that point and tell them "no." Why should you help them when they didn't believe in you? It's ok to feel that way, but don't let the hurt you felt turn you into the person you don't want to be: bitter and unforgiving. Be the person that your non-supporters weren't for you. Tell them your secrets, let them in on your journey. It feels much better to help than it does to hold a grudge.

Find Your Driving Force

Are you having trouble finding your passion? Do you feel like you don't have one? If you've made it this far in my book, you know that I had a lot of trouble finding my own passion. If that sounds like you, there are ways to figure out what drives you. Make a list of the things that you would like to do as a career. It can be as long or as short as you like. Close your eyes for a few minutes and picture yourself doing each thing on your list. Does it make you happy? Can you see yourself doing it for the long haul? If so, circle it. If not, cross it out.

Research the market for the circled items on your list. What do you need to do in order to make it happen for yourself? Do you need classes? What will it cost? How long will it take? Is there a market for it?

Look at your list again and cross out any items that don't meet your needs or that you don't feel are right for you.

Narrow your list down to two or three items if you have more than three. Of the items left on your list, which ones will provide you with the life you want? Take into account what you want your life to look like. Do you want to travel? Spend time with family? Work as few hours as possible? Where do you see yourself in five years? Ten? Which items will meet all of your personal goals? Perhaps you can combine a few items to make it unique to you.

Let's say you like to organize, but you also like Feng Shui and gardening. Those can all be combined into one business. Have your organizing as the selling point and add on Feng Shui to deepen the services and make your offering unique. Offer gardening as an added bonus to make the home stunning inside *and* out. There are many ways you could do this and every other idea you may have to make your passion your work and your life.

Keep in mind that not all ideas pan out, and that's ok. This is life, and life is a process, an exploration, and it is *meant* to change. I had the idea for an organizing business, but it didn't pan out for me. I hired a life coach who helped a lot with figuring out how to start a business I was passionate about. I was on my way to figuring out how I would start my organizing business when I discovered it wasn't something I could see myself doing for the long haul. All of the tasks my life coach had me do made me realize that I wasn't ready to run my own business, nor was I passionate enough about the organizing business. I still hadn't figured out what my passion truly was. I came to the conclusion that it wasn't right for me, and that's when I took my day job in the factory.

Life Coaches

Hiring a life coach was a great decision. I highly recommend it. The one I hired had me do personal tasks and inventories to figure out what I wanted to do. At the time, I thought I still wanted to massage. Then I explored my interest in organizing with Feng Shui. Finally, I decided to quit my massage job and work in the factory. I recently went through all of the tasks the life coach prompted me to do and found that writing was listed all over the place. I didn't even mention it to my coach. I guess I wasn't ready to take the leap or that it just wasn't on my radar as a possibility. I believe that your passion reveals itself when you aren't looking so hard. By that I mean, it will fall into your lap when you are ready for it. Remember, I took courses on writing, self-published and wrote many unfinished books. None of the things I did were aligned with writing until now. In the back of my mind, I always knew it was my passion but didn't know what to do with it. When you figure out what your passion is, be patient, the right materials and courses will fall into your lap. It might take you longer to find your passion, like me, but it will happen. Keep the faith!

Your Heart Says It All

Listen to your heart when it comes to your passion and ask for signs from God or whatever higher power you believe in. Steer clear of courses promising to make you rich in thirty days. I know how tempting it is to fall for ads like that. I've been burned by those before. Do your research before spending any money. I like to find reviews that are not on the actual site. Obviously, the course or product isn't going to list bad reviews on their site, so you need to find other sources. I do an online search for reviews of whatever I am interested in and read through at least fifty of them, good *and* bad. I don't make a decision until I read enough thorough reviews. Once you've read a bunch of reviews and feel like you want to go through with it, ask your higher power for a sign. You need to be specific when asking for signs. I like to talk to God. I let him know that I am dense when it comes to noticing signs, so it needs to be a big flashy one that I wouldn't miss.

Sounds funny, but when I've asked for signs in the past, I got them, but I would question whether they were signs or not. I learned to ask for something I wouldn't mistake for coincidence. I also like to let it marinate for a while. If I am meant to take the course or buy the product, I won't be able to stop thinking about it. If I forget about it after a few days, then it wasn't meant for me.

Even if you research and think about the decisions you are making, in the end, you still have to take risks. Invest in yourself. Life is meant to be enjoyed. Everyone needs to take time for their own happiness. If you don't invest in you, you won't ever get to live your best life.

Personality Traits

Take some time to learn about yourself as well. I love to take personality tests. They are great for getting to know who you are and further understand how you operate. I like one called 16 Personalities. 16 Personalities gets really deep into figuring out who you are and what makes you tick. It's based on the Myers-Briggs personality types. I am an INFJ, the advocate or counselor. I found out so much about myself with this test. It's amazing how accurate it is. They give you an in-depth report about your personality: it tells you about career, relationships and parenting style. It's a really good reference to keep on hand for when you are changing things in your life. You can refer back to it any time you want. It's good to know how you deal with people in your personal life as well as in your career so you can work on your weaknesses as well as your strengths.

Put in the time and effort to make your dream come true, you will thank yourself later. Putting in the time now will pay off tremendously in the future. Don't worry about getting off track, it happens to all of us. Dust yourself off, get back up and start fresh. If you need a day to rejuvenate, take it. I wouldn't take more than a day or two because if you do, you may never pick it back up. Focus on yourself and your healing, and take it one day at a time. Every day you wake up is a blessing; be grateful for that blessing, and live your life to its fullest. Truly follow your dreams. Someone else may have a similar idea or passion, but only you have your story. Your story is unique, your dream is unique and your passion is unique. You are the only person that can make your passion a reality, and your passion has the potential to make this world better for us all.

Kahlil Gibran wrote: "he who requires urging to do a noble act will never accomplish it." This couldn't have been truer for me. I spent the first several years of my life searching for someone to validate me, but once I found what I was passionate about, simply living was no longer a struggle. My passion gives me more room to perform my noble acts, being better for me, for my mom, for my daughter, for you. I finally feel like I can make an impact on the world and help people like you who are still struggling.

Epilogue

Man wants to know that his life has somehow counted.

—Ernest Becker

My life has been a roller coaster of highs and lows. I have made many bad decisions. Those decisions could have put me in jail, the hospital or worse; I could be dead. I spent time with drug dealers in a crack house. I drove drunk. I slept with random men. What was I thinking? Clearly, I *wasn't* thinking. I merely wanted to feel something. I am thankful every day that I didn't end up dead. I used to think, "Why couldn't I have been born into a rich family?" "Why couldn't I have a less argumentative dad and daughter?" "Why did I get depression and addiction issues?" "What would my life be like had I made different choices?" If I was born into a rich family, I may not have learned the value of money. If I had relatives who didn't argue, I may not have learned patience and understanding. If I didn't become depressed and have addiction issues, I wouldn't be writing this book or sharing my story. Had I made different choices, who knows where I would be? I could be living like royalty, or I could be homeless. But there is no point in dwelling on what "could have been" because "what is" is so much better. This is who I am, who I choose to be, and that person is amazing.

In this lifetime, I have learned patience, trust, understanding and how to love myself. I've been through a great deal of pain and have come out the other side stronger and more powerful. I am grateful for all of the things I have gone through, because if I hadn't gone through it, I would not be who I am today. I can finally say that I am truly happy with my life and with myself.

If you have battled depression and addiction like I have; what have *you* learned from that journey? I have discovered who I am and how I want to live my life. I have found my passion and am creating the life of my dreams.

So many of us go through times like that in our lives, and some of us don't make it through with our lives in-tact. I want to change that. I was lucky to make it out the other side alive. I want you to be able to say the same. No one has a perfect life. Our lives are all perfectly messy. We have ups and downs, happy days and sad days, good days and bad days. Sometimes we are thrown a giant curveball because the universe wants to see how we handle it. It is up to you how you handle curve-balls. You can let them claim your life, fall into a pit of despair, or you can tell the universe, "I got this."

When you are feeling down, remember that you are not alone. I can't say that enough. I lived that way for so long, alone and not letting anyone know I needed them. The best thing you can do for yourself is to tell someone, anyone, that you need them. Not everyone will be willing to help, but someone will. I will. It won't be easy. It will feel strange. Take a chance on you, let me help you. To me, the worst feeling in the world is loneliness. Loneliness makes depression worse.

Loneliness makes addiction worse. Reach out. Call a friend. Get yourself a hobby.

Depression is an ugly demon. It can make us harm ourselves, or others, hide from the world, never leave our homes. You never really know what to expect from day to day; depression is unpredictable. There are good days and bad days: exactly as life is like for someone without depression. The difference is that our bad days are really bad; we don't know how to deal with the sadness, and this makes our bad days worse than other people's bad days.

I don't tell many people about myself. There is so much judgment in the world, and it is a scary thing to open yourself up to other people's scrutiny. And it can be hard to find like-minded people, people who will love and accept you, no matter what. I wrote this book so that I could release the pain and fear that were keeping me stuck in patterns I no longer want to control me AND to reach out to other people who are going through similar experiences. Sometimes we need a friend to listen and not offer advice or their judgment. You may have to look outside of your circle of friends for that; find Facebook groups to join or classes to take. Through the groups and classes, I met a lot of people who accept me for who I am, who support me.

So, how do we learn to accept who we are? It is a learning process. For so long, I hated myself; I thought I wasn't good enough, but through my journey of self-discovery, I learned to love who I am. I learned that I am perfect the way I am, even if it *is* a bit messy.

Notes

If you or someone you know suffers from depression with thoughts of suicide there are many resources available.

Suicide Hotline: 1-800-273-8255
Suicide Text Hotline: 741741
Suicide Prevention: www.asfsp.org

About the Author

Rikki Meister has a passion for helping people. She is a former elementary teacher and massage therapist. Through her writing, she is able to help many people get through the darkness and into the light. Rikki loves to transform lives through self-help and self-care. She is a certified Akashic Records reader and Tarot/ Angel card reader. Connect with Rikki at www.mysticaladdict. com You can also connect on Facebook @rikkimeisterauthor to find out about upcoming books and courses.

Rikki lives in a small town in Minnesota with her amazing daughter, Riley, and her sweet cat, Lily.

Coming Soon

The Mystical Addict Book
A book about all things mystical and magical. Learn about crystals, meditating, tarot/angel cards, psychic abilities, akashic records and much more. The name of book is to be determined as of the publication of this book.

Surviving Narcissism
A true story of how Rikki survives childhood with a narcissistic dad only to have a child with the same tendencies. Learn how to deal with narcissism in many ways and keep your sanity.

Isle of Beauty
A fiction fantasy series based around fairies and crystals. The main character has just found out that she is a fairy. She must leave her home to join a school for teen fairies and learn about fairy magic and crystal healing powers. Amber soon learns that her mother is leading a coven of fairies to help protect the school against the evil force trying to destroy all fairy kind.

Courses Coming Soon

Perfectly Messy Life Coaching Program
A 30-day course teaching you how to live with depression and addiction. Every day will bring a new challenge to complete. We all have a perfectly messy life; learn to accept who you are and live a life with passion and fulfillment.

Beginner Crystal Course
Learn how crystals can help with ailments, manifesting and much more. Learn how to use and take care of crystals.

CPSIA information can be obtained
at www.ICGtesting.com
Printed in the USA
LVHW050009240919
631983LV00003B/546/P

9 781640 856738